CHAPEL
into
CHURCH

HOW DENTON CHAPEL BECAME ST. LAWRENCE'S CHURCH

by

The REVEREND A. JOHN WARD, B.D.
Rector of St. Lawrence's

1973

CHAPEL INTO CHURCH

Printed by
J. Andrew & Co. Ltd., Whitelands Road, Ashton-under-Lyne

The Oldest known picture of Denton Chapel, drawn in 1796.
By permission of The British Museum.

CONTENTS

CHAPTER FOUR

THE FIRST RECTOR

CHAPTER FIVE
THE OLD CHURCH IS ENLARGED

ILLUSTRATIONS

ACKNOWLEDGEMENTS

I would like to thank Miss L. E. Middleton of Hyde for permission to quote extensively from her father's books. The Editor of the Reporter Group of Newspapers, the Trustees of the British Museum, the County Archivists of Cheshire and Lancashire, the Staffs of the Local History Library, St. Peter's Square, Chetham's Library, the Rylands Library, the Manchester Diocesan Registry and Miss Joan Wharton, Librarian of Denton Public Library have also given me much kind assistance and permission to quote from documents in their keeping. Mr. Richard Greswell, Mr. Burley Key and others mentioned in the footnotes have also made information available to me. Lastly, Mrs. Wynne Walker of Denton has typed the manuscript with great care and attention. Any mistakes must be regarded as mine. May those who follow in my footsteps correct them.

A.J.W.

INTRODUCTION

FIVE men have played a major part in recording the history of Denton. They are Oliver Heywood, John Booker, Samual Hadfield, Thomas Middleton and Burley Key of Haughton Green.

Heywood wrote the life of John Angier, who was Denton's godly, puritan minister from 1632 to 1677. Booker wrote a History of the Ancient Chapel of Denton after visiting it and taking careful notes in 1854. Middleton first published his Annals of Hyde and District (1899); followed it with the History of Hyde (1901), then published an Historical Sketch of Denton Old Church in 1931 (to commemorate the four hundredth anniversary of the foundation of the church) and finally brought out his large History of Denton and Haughton in 1936. Burley Key is our present historian, patiently amassing a wealth of information about Denton and Haughton's past. We owe him an immense debt.

But what of Samuel Hadfield? He was born on June 4th, 1825, in a cottage in Old Broom Lane, Haughton, in which he continued to live all his life as his father had done before him. His father lived to be over eighty, father and son tenanting the same house for more than a century.[1]

He was baptized by The Reverend William Greswell on October 16th, 1825, in Denton Chapel and in his early teens began work as a weaver at Kingston Mills. Middleton tells us that he later became a hatter like his father, John Hadfield, but at the time of his marriage he was an overlooker of a power loom.

The wedding on January 14th, 1854 was the very first to take place in Christ Church. Samuel, twenty-eight years old, married Susannah Cheetham, who was thirty and worked as a weaver. They had two sons and a daughter, all christened in St. Lawrence's – William Greswell (1856–1908), Edward Greswell (1858–1890) and Jane (1860–1937). In naming the boys their father paid a noteable compliment to the Greswell family and in particular to two clerical gentlemen whom we shall meet in these pages. Jane, who was a Sunday School teacher for many years at St. Lawrence's is still remembered with great affection.

Middleton tells us that at eighteen years of age Samuel Hadfield began contributing articles to the local press on historical subjects.[2] He continued to do so for fifty-eight years and so became by far the most important local historian Denton has ever had and its first indigenous one. He never published a book but most of the articles he wrote for newspapers are still extant.

[1] Middleton: *History of Denton and Haughton.* Page 134.
[2] Ibid: page 133. He often writes under the pen-name of "Scrutator."

Hadfield's social position was that of the working-class, skilled artisan. He was not the sort of man to publish books, but he certainly helped two others to publish theirs. When The Reverend John Booker visited Denton, Hadfield supplied him with a good deal of information and probably escorted him round the town. But it was Middleton, who knew him when he was elderly, who owes the most gigantic debt to him. "It was a treat to listen to his stories," he tells us,[1] "and I have spent many hours in his old cottage whilst he conjured up visions of other days." Without doubt, Thomas Middleton would have found the task of writing his History of Denton and Haughton infinitely more difficult without Hadfield's assistance. He had witnessed so much. He knew Parr Greswell and four of his sons. He knew Thomas Farthing, Walter Nicol and Charles James Bowen. He saw Denton Chapel restored internally in 1859 and externally in 1862. He saw it enlarged in 1873 and heard Bishop Fraser's sermon at the re-dedication. He saw Christ Church Schools and Christ Church itself built. He saw St. Lawrence's school built. He knew the Iron School at Haughton Green; he saw St. Mary's built – and much, much else.

From his cottage in Old Broom Lane he sold local papers. You could get your copy of the *Ashton Standard* there on a Saturday morning and he acted as an agent receiving advertisements. In 1888, his son Edward married Sarah Ellor in St. Lawrence's. By then he had become a hatter and was to live another thirteen years. The Reverend David Rowe took his funeral on July 25th, 1901 and he was buried in St. Lawrence's churchyard.

Conscious of his enormous debt, Middleton paid a tribute to Samuel Hadfield in his Annals of Hyde, published three years before he died. It is a magnificent example of a glorious purple passage – an amusingly patronising tone running through it. Nevertheless it was sincerely meant and deserves to be quoted in full.

> "In ancient days every village had its minstrel, its village poets, who made its lore, its sages, its songs of village deeds, and then sang them in the tap-room of the village inn. The puritan may sneer at this, but after all the man was the legitimate descendant of the old-time minstrel whom iron-handed custom had driven from his high estate. Even the village poet has left us now, but his descendant still lives on, in another shape perhaps, but yet the link in the chain that binds the past with the present. The modern minstrel is the antiquary, and he wants finding. Unlike the ancient representative of his order, he does not wander with "his roundelays from door to door". He thinks he would not be welcome and so he stays at home.

[1] Ibid: page 134.

"Such a character dwells in our midst today, and his work deserves recognition, because he does what will in days to come be looked on as a public service. He gathers and stores the records of the past. He does it with no thought of reward, he does it because he loves the task, the minstrel spirit is in him still; though the prosaic 19th century swings around him. Mr. Samuel Hadfield, of Haughton, is a "character" of whom a volume might be written. He is a hale old fellow of 79,[1] and in his youth he was a spinner. Afterwards he joined the band of "jolly hatters" for which Denton has long been famed. But he loved the past, the great old histories, the "legends and traditions with their voices from afar off." He loved them all; he treasured them in his heart, and longed to hand them down. In this love of ancient things he is typical of many another cotton worker of a past generation.

"For years he has contributed fugitive essays on local history topics to the papers of the district – *The North Cheshire Herald, The Ashton Herald, The Ashton Reporter, The Hyde and Denton Chronicle, The Denton and Haughton Examiner* – the last two now defunct. His writings show a rare and racy literary style, and are of more than average merit. Besides the above topics they include character sketches and descriptive rambles of the district. There is a decided literary flavour in all his work, and a collection of his pieces should prove of value in the future.

"Mr. Hadfield's writing days are now almost over, but still he is a reliable source of information and folk-lore. His mind is stocked and every article is catalogued and in order. His home is clean and neat, with a neatness and a cleanliness that belongs to other days; it is antiquity itself. He has bits of oak, the walls are covered with illustrations and prints of every intellectual order, bishops, statesmen, places of antiquity, old halls and manors, and famous men of past times. His library consists of thousands on thousands of newspaper cuttings. He has every scrap of writing that deals with the local past. He has every sermon preached by the late Bishop of Manchester (Fraser) and many another literary treasure from the same master mind. His cottage is a veritable curiosity and a paragon of order. Every paper is docked and ticketed. Every scrap has its place and the necessary document is forthcoming whenever it is required. He is like some grey magician, some Merlin of the olden times at whose summons comes up from the dream mists of the past, pictures of all that has

[1] Wrong! He was 74 at the time this was written!

been, pictures of the sacred memories of these parts, and in them live and move and speak, the men, the figures, and the voices of the mighty host of local forms who have long ago been still. It is a treat in these days to see a character like our antiquary. God grant his race may never die."[1]

A good example of the sort of article Hadfield would write appeared in *The Ashton Weekly Reporter* on June 13th, 1857. It is called "Denton and its Vicinity" and is well worth re-publishing. At the end is simply the letter 'H' as signature. We cannot be certain that it stood for Hadfield but we do know that the six hour walk was enjoyed by a party, one or two of whom supplied historical details which only a local historian could have known. It is probable, therefore, that he was one of the party.

Interior view of Samuel Hadfield's Cottage.

"Christ Church, standing on the south side of the Manchester Road, in a spacious and neatly-kept graveyard, is a pretty specimen of a small village church, in the Gothic style, prevalent in the 14th century. The summit of the spire attains an altitude of 140 feet. The edifice was consecrated with much eclat in October, 1853. The

[1] Middleton: *Annals of Hyde and District* (1899).

schools, neat erections also of stone, are situated on the opposite side of the highway, fronted by a small garden plot. In Windmill Lane, nestling under the shadow of the steeple, stands, in the "course of erection," a square block of mottled-brick and mortar, guiltless of any attempt at architectural embellishment or beauty. Our native simplicity was sore puzzled in attempting to divine the status of its future occupants, and just as we are setting it down for a public-house our ciceronë astonishes us by asserting it was intended for the parsonage house.[1]

"Denton, in this respect, akin to most country places, is a long straggling village, chiefly bordering on the Ashton and Stockport Road. The Manchester and Hyde Road, which crosses it at right angles, is also becoming margined with buildings. Near the east end of Christ churchyard is Bridgehouse Fold, the present dwelling-house superseding a few years ago a substantial farmhouse dated 1651, the entrance door of which exhibited loops or slots, through which, according to tradition, musketry were once fired when the place was held in a state of siege by the tenants or occupants against the owners. In 1597 Grace Bridghous, widow, was a Denton rate-payer, and in 1655, Thomas Leez paid rates for Bridghous. The name of Robert Bridghous appears inscribed as a warden on the chapel bell, with the date of 1715. The last of the Bridges, as the name was contracted, sold the estate some years ago to Mr. William Taylor. Fronting the Hyde Road is also the residence of Horace Jackson, of Denton and Hyde, a saddler, and poet of some local note. Public-house signs are frequently an index to the characteristics of a village in more respects than one. Here is "Sodger Dick", commemorating, we suppose, some local aspirant once fired with military enthusiasm. The original, we learned, was a curious blade, who, many years since, delighted in singing a rhyming narrative of a soldier's adventures, the burden of the chorus interrogating –

> Don't you know me by my scars,
> Just returning from the wars?

Here also is the sign of the "Jolly Hatters" rather out of keeping, we suspect, with these degenerate days, and indicative rather of the sprees and well-doings of a generation gone by. Twenty or thirty years ago the Denton hatters were, to a certainty, a jolly race of fellows, on padding days at least. When returning from Stockport, with wallets

---

[1] A ciceronë is a guide who explains antiquities. Nineteenth century journalists loved to show off their knowledge of words. The heavy, involved style spoils this article. (Christ Church Rectory was demolished in 1966–7).

on their shoulders, they might be seen shuffling homewards, led up by a muffled fidler, scraping some attempt at a favourite tune. Sad reverses have since passed over the trade; nevertheless, we met many strapping young fellows, sporting shining hats and white aprons, evidencing that the hatting trade has not yet entirely departed from the district, although "ichabod" is unmistakeably written on its former prosperity.

"The old chapel is a pleasing specimen of the half-timbered ecclesiastical edifice, and was built in 1531–2, and dedicated to St. James. The chapelyard has recently been enlarged, and tastefully planted with yews, evergreen shrubs and various young forest trees. The entrance on the south side is through a picturesque lych-gate, of rude workmanship, built, as the villagers tell you, with the sole aid of a sledge-hammer and cold chisel. This shed, or canopy, as its Saxon name (lych, a dead body) imports, was used as a resting-place for the coffin until the officiating clergyman came to precede the corpse to church, the while repeating the commencement of that impressive service, the office for the burial of the dead. In the grave-yard are various funereal inscriptions appertaining to the seventeenth century, the oldest extant simply inscribed "IH 1674;" this is eighteen years anterior to the oldest existing register deposited in the chapel. A flat stone, palisaded round, commemorates the Rev. William Parr Greswell, 63 years minister of the chapel, who died January, 1854, in the 89th year of his age, as also various members of his family. Another stone remembers John Pollit, a former clerk and schoolmaster, who died October 24th, 1854, aged 50 years; whilst another indicates the last resting place of a worthy man killed June 30th, 1856, by a coalpit explosion, John Merick, of Haughton, aged 36 years. The teachers and scholars of Denton and Haughton Church Sunday Schools presented the tablet as a testimony of respect for his valuable services as superintendent at the Haughton school. Internally, the chapel is divided by a spacious aisle, the pews radiating to the north being accounted the Denton side, whilst those on the south appertain unto Haughton. The pulpit is fixed nearly midway against the north wall, and is dated 1659. There is also a singing loft or gallery, erected in 1728, in which is placed a small organ commensurate with the size of the edifice. Ascending the wooden turret which crowns the western apex, we found the bell inscribed with the names of the wardens, and the year of casting, 1715. This bell, of humble proportions, bears the euphonious appellation of "Owd Peg," in supposed commemoration of the wife of a former sexton.[1] Moses Hardy, the present venerable gravedigger, &c., is well known in the neighbourhood, and never, perhaps, except on the Sabbath, owing to his fondness for "working stript", can he be met with the whole of his clothes on his back at one time. Tradition represents the frame-work of the chapel as having been formed and erected in Holt Wood, appertaining to the Hydes Hall estate, Denton. A document, in possession of the Earl of Wilton, states it to have been Hibbert Wood. The former place is identifiable, the latter has not yet been made out. As the chapel was erected by the Hydes and Hollands, most probably the timber was grown in Holt Wood. Formerly, with an exception or two, the edifice was filled with low forms with diminutive backs, made of massive black oak, on which the congregation sat, with their feet immersed in rushes. The Minister, for a Sunday or two preceding the wake, yearly gave notice that the rushbearing and flowering would take place as usual. The Haughton manufacturers getting on in business, and waxing proud, in 1768 they pewed their side of the chapel, and deridingly designated the Denton side "th'owd bedstocks." Afterwards the Denton manu-facturers, prospering in like manner, got their side pewed, and thus erased the stigma for ever; at least, so avers an aged inhabitant of the locality. A passing glance is administered upon the long rambling erection of old cottages adjoining the yard on the western side. So long and continuous a range of thatched dwellings are seldom met with, cottages of that description being generally detached, and isolated from each other by garden-plots.

"Leaving the graveyard, we take down a narrow and no ways inviting lane, dignified with the appellation of the "Town Lane" and soon reach a few paltry dwellings, ennobled with the distinctive name, rights, and privileges, of "the city." The denisons of this favoured pale are regarded, as our guide informed us in the elegant Doric of the locality, as "full bred uns, wi' sengle koms, un red deofyers." The translation we leave to the cock-fighters and linguists of the South Lancashire dialects. Anon, we come on the left to a substantial yeomanry-dwelling with projecting centre, occupied by a seated porch and closet above it, inscribed KEL. JL 1720. This house was erected by one of the many branches of the Lees family in Denton, and still remains in their occupation. The outbuildings are of a more ancient date, and have a framework of timber. A little further up the lane, on the opposite side are the works of Mr. William Cooke, hat manu-

[1] This is an astonishing explanation of the name "Owd Peg," but it could be right.

facturer, with a stone recording the initials of the builders of the original dwelling-house, and the year of our Lord "SMC. 1697." Still further up the lane, on the right side, are the works of Mr. Henry Booth, also a silk-hat manufacturer, converted from a dwelling-house, originally erected by a branch of the prolific Lees family; over the porch the incised stone bears a plume of feathers, and "TLEL 1667." In the 17th century this house was the scene of a touching event. The Lees had some relatives in London, who migrated thence out of the way of the great plague, when, soon after settling here, three of them took the infection, brought down in a box of clothes, and died. So great was the fear of contagion that the bodies were refused interment in Denton chapel yard, and were subsequently buried in a field a short distance from the house, the precise spot near an old pit-stead being still pointed out.[1]

"An undulating field path leads into Windmill Lane, a beerhouse marking the site of an ancient mill which conferred the designation on the lane. Denton Hall is a long post and petrel edifice, supposed to have been erected about the close of the 16th century. A family bearing the local name resided in Denton as early as the 13th century, and about 1322, Margaret, the daughter and heiress of Sir A. Denton, Knt., of Denton, married John Shoresworth, Esq.; and their daughter and sole heiress, Margaret, married Sir William Holland and conveyed the Denton estates to that family, from whom they have descended to their present noble owner. This was once a large farm, but of late years has been much subdivided, only about 80 acres now remaining attached to the hall. The scenery from this place is agreeably diversified with hill and dale, meadow and plantation. Close by are several denes and dingles, filled with plantations and underwood, one of which probably gave the prefix to Den-ton, that is, the enclosed place in the vale. Danes-head-bank, a short distance from the hall, seems, in the 11th century, to have been equal, if not superior in importance to Denton proper. There are danes, or denes also in Audenshaw, Gorton and Droylsden. In the distance lies Holland Moors, indicating the locale of the Denton waste of which 292 acres were enclosed in the time of Queen Elizabeth. A pleasant stretch across a couple of meadows brings one to Hyde Hall, so named from an old family once resident here. The edifice has been built at different periods, the most ancient apparently in the 16th century. Affixed in front are a sundial and the arms of the Hydes, dated 1625. The estate is 140 acres in extent, with

[1] Middleton, page 117-118.

out-housing of corresponding capacity, all, except a bay or two, inscribed "R.M.H. 1687," of recent erection; forming, in the whole, a large, square, and compact farm yard.

Emerging from the fold into an occupation lane, bound in by unclipt hedges, rich with the fragrance of sweet willow and the snowy blossoms of the hawthorn, strongly reminding us of one of Burn's sweetest lays, the path bends down to the banks of the Tame, and gently we tread on the rich green sward variegated with its myriads of inimitable flowers. The banks and slopes are covered with bluebells and yellow crowfoot, or "buttercups", as the latter are more poetically than truthfully named from the false supposition of their imparting the yellow tinge to butter, when, in reality, cattle always avoid them on account of their biting propensity. Butterflies are sporting from flower to flower, and the sun emits warmth sufficient to cheer and invigorate without overpowering the pedestrian. Bredbury Church, Werneth Lowe, and a profusion of landscape beauties, are spread out around. The fences are interspersed with shady trees, fast clothing in full maturity of verdure. Orchards are gay and beautiful with the blush of apple blossoms. The Tame runs below and Arden Hall rears its ancient walls and octagonal tower before us.

"A short distance from the river side, beneath a shady copse, we were shown a scarce variety of moth or butterfly, said to be confined to a circuit of one or two score yards in extent, naturalists coming as far as from Oldham, in order to obtain specimens for preservation. The botanist may be pleased to know that several scarce plants grow in these parts. In preference to their formidable Latin names, we give them in plain English – wall-rue and hart's-tongue are found in the moat wall, broad leaved hitchwort in the wear, and adder's tongue and moonwart in the meadow to the west of Arden Hall; bird's cherry abounds in Reddish Wood; geranium, milkwort, scabious, and wood betony in the "Twenty-Acre"; and bugle and viper's grass, alias forget-me-not, in the wood, both near to Denton Hall.

"Traversing a delightful path, parallel to the river on the north side, crossing the stream at Reddish printworks, and returning on the south side, we enter a cottage garden, to look at a thick and curious ivystem, forming an arch five or six feet high, and then grasping a gable wall. Evidently some small building or pantry against which it clustered has been removed, and thus its present shape acquired. Passing through Arden Wood, which every year admits more daylight, seated on a gentle eminence called Castle Hill, stands Harden or Arden Hall, probably occupying the site of a more ancient and perhaps fortified edifice. The moat carries us back to that distant period when life and property were constantly in jeopardy. The drawbridge is supplanted by permanencies, one of brick and the other of stone. The water is superseded by fruit trees, strongly illustrative of the present secure and happier times, when every Englishman's cot is his castle. The age-tinted edifice is in a state of dilapidation, and rapidly sinking into decay. In a few years hence, if no friendly hand arrests the spoilations of time, nought will remain save a mouldering heap of ruins. On the front of the structure are the family arms and crest, an ancient clock and a modern sundial dated 1796, and on a waterspout the inscription "RA 1597.IA 1597.H.A." Entering the courtyard, almost expecting to issue forth a goodly array of lordly knights and fair dames mounted on palfreys, but instead we are greeted with signs of desolation and woe. The very threshold is over-grown with docks, and thistles, and brambles. A green shrub waves its branches on the roof, whilst ivy pierces the crevices and casements, and luxuriates in the dormitories – fit companions for widowhood.

"A short walk conducts to Arden mills, now used as a paper-manufactory, but formerly a corn mill, and visited in 1812 by the Luddites. At that time, one Nathan Howard acted as salesman in dispensing with the flour, &c. at low prices. The military arrived from Stockport when Howard took the mill dam, and, though fired at, escaped and emigrated from the country. Traversing the banks of the river on the Cheshire side, and then a short rural lane, we come to a quarry of the old red sandstone, and stand on the precipitous margin of the stream, listening to the gentle rushing of the waters below. "Oh! for a loll on those grassy banks, beneath that oak tree's canopy, with a book in hand," cries one of the party; "or rather with a maiden by your side," enjoins another. A wooden footbridge spans the river, whereby Haughton Dale is gained. Shortly, and unexpectedly, we come upon a palatial-like edifice, erected – but not yet opened – by James Walton, Esq., of Haughton Dale Mills. This beautiful structure is built of iron, and internally cased with wood. It is 24 yards by 12, eight windows in length and four in breadth, and two storeys high, supported by seven pillars each. The floor of the lower room is tiled, and the upper one of wood, and about 14 feet high. The internal furniture and fittings are not yet completed. The estimated cost is £2,000. The design and ornamentation are very pleasing, and con-stitute it an elegant multum in parvo, it being intended for use as a day and Sunday-school, with divine service on Sabbath evenings, and also as a mechanics' institution. The ventilation appears sadly defective, but may be remedied by means of the aperture between the external iron and the inside woodwork, at least, if the panels are distinct from each other. They might be perforated alternately near the floor and near the ceiling, the lower admitting the cold air, and the upper permitting the escape of the heated and impure. Delighted with this bright example of an employer's attention to the mental and spiritual wants of his workpeople, we earnestly prayed that other masters might at once "go and do likewise."[1] Leaving to the right "Clark's Arms," which is situated on the highest land in Haughton (high-town) and also on the most elevated point in the very extensive parish of Manchester, we pass through Haughton Green, and behold numbers of dwellings with cracked walls, and some uninhabited, caused by subsidence of the earth through mining operations underneath. Haughton pinfold is a small circular building, insulated by the road side. Haughton Hall, erected at different periods, was once infested with "fearin", in the shape of a lady haunting the premises after dark; but as our informant remarked, "they catcht boggart, un then o'ur reet." Calling at a friends' house after six hours' tramping, it needs no bondsman to certify that the whole party eat like a lot of thrashers. The grey twilight had mantled round the house-tops, Christ Church spire was left in the distance, and the journey homewards was enlivened by pleasing chit-chat and such melody as the company were capable of."

St. Lawrence's church is 442 years old, but this book only covers 85 years – from 1791 to 1876. I have chosen this period because it was a crucial one in the church's long life-span. During those years the old tudor building was firstly, saved from collapse; secondly, restored and thirdly, enlarged. Moreover, it was during this period that Denton Chapelry became St. Lawrence's Parish.

The debt I owe to Middleton, Hadfield and Booker is one I am only too happy to acknowledge and constant references to their works will be found in these pages, even though a good deal of new material which has never before been published has come to light. Hadfield's newspaper articles are particularly informative, but so also is Middleton if read very carefully. His History of Denton and Haughton reminds one of a chest of drawers stuffed full of old clothes of every description. You open it and find one bedsock in this drawer and its pair in that! The information is

---

[1] This is, of course, the famous Iron School which Walton had just built.

usually there, but it is scattered through the pages and without an index to guide you it can easily be missed. This is because it is a collection of newspaper articles rather than a book in the usual sense of the word. Nevertheless, it is an absolutely essential, basic work for any study of Denton's history.

On April 6th, 1873 Bishop Fraser dedicated the enlarged portions of St. Lawrence's church. On April 8th, 1973, we commemorated this event. It is amazing that this fascinating building – Denton's oldest – still plays such an important role in the life of the community. But it does and it is no mere museum piece. It is the home – the open, welcoming home – of a living, Christian fellowship, a stronghold of the love and goodness of Jesus Christ, Our Lord.

A.J.W.

Easter 1973.

CHAPTER ONE

THE OLD CHAPEL SURVIVES

IN 1791 William Parr Greswell was given his first – and only living. It was Denton, together with its neighbour Haughton, two rough, uncivilised villages on the Lancashire side of the Tame.

What a big responsibility for a young man of twenty-six who had been ordained only two years and whose experience of the parochial ministry was limited to the one short curacy served at Blackley. How grateful, one wonders, did he feel to the first Earl of Wilton, his patron? Denton, a chapel of ease to Manchester parish church, was a poor living. Parr Greswell and his wife faced a certain amount of very real hardship, but fortunately this was alleviated to some extent by his Lordship's loan of Wilton House[1] on Ashton Road, which the Earl built for him and allowed him to occupy whilst he remained Perpetual Curate of Denton Chapel. Even so, to augment his stipend he had to open a little grammar school in his home for the sons of local gentry, and it is said that Mrs. Greswell was sometimes seen doing her housework with a baby tied in her lap.

A Stranger discovers the Chapel

In 1796, when Parr Greswell had been Incumbent for five years, a Mr. William Orme passed through the village. The old chapel intrigued him so much that he sat down and drew the first picture of it that has yet come to light and sent it to the December edition of the famous *Gentleman's Magazine* with the following note:

"Enclosed you will receive a drawing (Plate 1) of an old chapel at Denton, a long straggling village on the Lancashire side of the Tame, about seven miles from Manchester. On one of the windows there is the date of 1531, and it appears to have undergone no material alteration since that time, except the addition of a new balcony and other necessary improvements of paint and whitewash. The old yew tree is in a very decayed state, and gives an air of antiquity to the whole. Were it not for the tomb-stones it would pass for one of the old black and white halls so common in this part of the country.

Yours etc. WILLIAM ORME."

How peaceful! How delightful! Yet this is very much an outsider's view, for behind the "air of antiquity" which seemed to please Mr. Orme so much lurked a terrible threat to the existence of the old chapel. It was the

---

[1] Now the surgery of Doctors P. Brodbin and C. A. O'Conner.

growing conviction that it had had its day. Most parishioners felt that it had come to the end of its useful life and should be demolished. But Parr Greswell did not agree.

Will Boney Come?

The news from abroad was alarming. "France," said Napoleon Bonaparte, "needs glorious deeds and hence war. She must be first among the states or she is lost." In March, 1802 England had concluded a peace with him at Amiens, but it did not last. The following year he gathered his army at Boulogne. A large number of flatboats were collected and troops trained to embark and disembark. Invasion fever swept England and Parliament passed "An Act to enable his Majesty more Effectually to provide for the Defence and Security of the Realm". This led to an important meeting in the Chapel on August 22nd, 1803, at which Mr. Parr Greswell presided. After discussion and fervently patriotic speeches "It was unanimously Resolved That an offer shall be made to the Lord Lieutenant of the County of 50 men to be armed and clothed at the joint Expense of the Townships of Denton and Haughton to serve agreeably to the Terms specified in the said Act".[1] The signature of William Parr Greswell, Minister of Denton, heads the list of 17 leading parishioners and we know from Middleton that the Volunteers (60 he says) "looked very smart in their uniform – red tunics, faced with blue and black breeches and leggings of the same colour. They were full of zeal for it was expected that Bonaparte with his invincible army, would land upon the coast of Kent before they were qualified to take the field and the Denton hatters felt that if there was to be any fighting they ought to have a hand in it."[2]

Most Mellifluous Music

Boney didn't come – and in 1805 Nelson defeated his navy at Trafalgar. By 1807 the men of Denton felt safe enough to disband the Volunteers and turn their attention to a matter which must have given them much pleasure, the purchase of the Chapel's first organ. Astonishingly the fund was oversubscribed! George Hyde Clarke gave £21 and the total was £175.16.6.[3] The cost of buying and setting up the organ in the gallery was £139.4.10 leaving £36.11.8 to be spent on something else. Mr. George Hyde Clarke suggested that it be used for erecting an altar and vestry in the Chapel[4] and a meeting held on Monday, September 14th, 1807 approved of this

[1] Church Register 1787–1812.
[2] Thomas Middleton: *History of Denton and Haughton* (1936), pp. 125–128. He gives a full and interesting account of the Volunteers with amusing stories, but unfortunately the "small book containing the particulars" to which he refers has disappeared from the church records.
[3] Middleton is wrong in saying £112.10.0. was collected (p. 73). That was the price of the actual instrument.
[4] Church Register 1787–1812.

suggestion readily, knowing that if the cost was more than £36 Mr. Hyde Clarke would pay the extra himself.[1]

The organ was placed in the middle of the gallery which had been built in 1728. Above the north side of this gallery is a window in the roof. The seats under it were reserved for "the free use of the present set of psalm-singers".[2] They sang in four-part harmony and how pleased they would be on May 10th, 1807 when the organ was played for the very first time by Joseph Sidebotham! It would seem a great improvement on what had gone before. The choir had been accompanied by village musicians playing various instruments. Often a solitary bassoon played the bass line an octave below the bass voices. A 'cello might play in unison with the bass voices, whilst a clarinet, flute or fiddler played the melody. In Denton, John and Nathan Sidebotham (Joseph's father and uncle) played violin and 'cello until the organ was installed.[3]

On the south side of the gallery we would find Mrs. Greswell with, perhaps, her eldest boys. Other distingished parishioners might be there too for the records said: "One pew to be assigned to the Minister's house and the rest such persons as will subscribe the largest sums towards augmenting the Minister's salary.[4]

What on earth were they doing buying an organ when they had not even got an altar? Undoubtedly the first organ was something of a novelty, a status symbol and therefore very popular, but in dealing with what was once a Puritan Chapel we must remember that the one item of ecclesiastical furniture of importance to Puritans was the pulpit. This was of dark oak and stood against the North wall half way down the Chapel. It bore the date 1659.[5] Very probably the seats did not face east as they do now. They may well have faced the pulpit, which means that those who sat in what is now the front of the nave would have had their backs to the east end. And what of the chancel? There was none! By "an altar and vestry" Mr. Hyde Clarke means an altar standing inside the small chancel we see in pictures of the church before its enlargement in 1873 and also a vestry on the north side. If this is correct, the following note from Booker begins to make sense:

"The chapel consists of a nave and chancel, the latter of very scanty proportions and of recent date added about the year 1800 by the

[1] Church Register 1787–1812, very faintly written note on an unnumbered left-hand page.
[2] Middleton: page 39. He gives their names in 1728. There were 41 of them, not counting the musicians!! (page 45). They could surely not all get into the north side of the gallery at once!
[3] Wainwright Manuscript.
[4] Ibid: page 39.
[5] The Revd. J. Booker: *History of the Ancient Chapel of Denton* (Chetham Society 1855), p. 43.

Revd. W. P. Greswell who on entering upon his Incumbency found neither chancel nor communion table; from which circumstances he drew the inference that the Presbyterian form of administering the Holy Communion had continued to prevail there up to that late period."[1]

The column of expenses "attending the Erection of an Altar and a Vestry in Denton Chapel" seems to bear out the suggestion that a chancel had to be built for the new altar. One item reads "Glazier's bill for Altar Window £1.5.0." However, a little vestry was also built at the same time, adjoining the north wall of the chapel. The column of expenses tells us there was a useful cupboard in it and an outside seat below the window. Altogether £55.4.4. was spent, so Mr. George Hyde Clarke supplied £18.12.8. from his own pocket.

A Good Stone Wall

Perhaps Parr Greswell had put the idea of the altar and chancel into Mr. Hyde Clarke's mind. Certainly something had roused Mr. Hyde Clarke to action, because on September 11th, 1809 he suggested to a meeting in the Chapel that a stone wall be built around the churchyard. There seems to have been some money to spare again, this time left over from the Napoleonic Volunteer subscription, and Mr. Hyde Clarke was willing "to make out whatever deficiency may remain and complete the erection of the said wall at his own proper cost and charge."[2] Once again Booker's account seems somewhat inaccurate, but it must be quoted in full:

"In this year (1810) the chapel yard was surrounded by a substantial stone wall at an expense of £182.18.10¾. The cost was defrayed by assessment of the inhabitants, each of the two townships contributing its quota.[3] The assessment having been found insufficient a voluntary subscription, headed by George Hyde Clarke Esq. with a donation of £40 was entered into, which completed the sum required."[4]

A Strong Letter to the Bishop

Yet in spite of all these improvements there is no doubt that Denton Chapel was very badly neglected by the Parishioners. The building as a

---

[1] Ibid: p. 41.
[2] Church Register 1787–1812. Before this a wooden fence had enclosed the churchyard. The Chapel Warden's account for 1793–4 contains the entry, "Fencing the chapel yard 1 shilling and 2½d." This means repairing part of the broken fence.
[3] The Church Register (1787–1812) does not say so. It speaks of "the residue of the volunteer subscription". It mentions no assessment.
[4] Revd. J. Booker: *A History of the Ancient Chapel of Denton* (Chetham Society, 1855), p. 121.

whole was in a dreadful state and Mr. Parr Greswell began to find his patience running out. Nevertheless, it is only after he has been Perpetual Curate for twenty-four years that he finally becomes exasperated and decides that he must make a complaint to his bishop. So on November 29th, 1815, he sat down and wrote a long letter to Dr. George Henry Law, D.D., Lord Bishop of Chester.[1] It is so important that it must be quoted in full:

"My Lord,

"It is my duty to place before your Lordship the following particulars relating to my Chapel of Denton with as little prolixity as the nature of the subject will admit.

"The Chapel is one of the most ancient specimens of wooden architecture remaining in these parts. It was probably erected circa 1530. It is consequently become very ruinous and requires constant expense and attention to keep it in any tolerable repair. The ancient mode of providing for these repairs is by a district Chapel rate levied on the inhabitants of Denton and Haughton in equal parts for that purpose. As this money is levied from the same sources as the Poor Rate, some indolent Chapel Wardens perhaps within these last 20 years procured these disbursements to be repaired out of the poor rates to save the trouble of a district collection. This course prevailed for a series of years without notice of its impropriety. But of late years these townships have employed standing Overseers of the poor who discharge this office not for an annual period merely but constantly in consideration of a salary paid them for that service. These factitious Officers by degrees growing indolent and contumacious have refused to reimburse the Chapel Wardens the sum advanced by them on chapel affairs. The late Chapel Wardens have in consequence declined to advance money for the necessary repairs of the edifice and hence its condition is in a rapid state of dilapidation. During the last winter it was actually dangerous to assemble in it for divine service. I have not been wanting, my Lord, in my duty of calling upon them earnestly to return to the ancient and only legal custom of a separate Chapel Rate. But as Chapel Wardens are still indolent, country lay payers Selfish, the custom grown almost obsolete and large contributions requisite, I have not yet been able to effect this necessary measure. To show how little assistance in this good work has been extended to me even by

[1] Denton Chapel has stood in three dioceses: the diocese of Lichfield from 1531–1541 when the diocese of Chester was created and from 1541–1847 in the diocese of Chester when the diocese of Manchester was formed.

Chapel Wardens themselves, I send the inclosed paper No. 1 being a notice whereby with consent of the then Wardens I procured a Vestry to be summoned August 20, 1814. When the day of assembling came not even my Chapel Wardens who sanctioned the summons met me and I was actually the only person who attended. Being desirous to prevent the like disappointment in future I again (form No. 2) procured a Vestry to be summoned for Easter Monday last when I knew the Wardens and lay payers must necessarily assemble for the election of new Officers for the year. I brought forward the business of Chapel repairs accordingly on that day and procured by a considerable majority an order (in form No. 3) for levying £100 in equal proportions on the Townships by a regular Chapel Rate which the new Chapel Wardens were directed to collect with all convenient speed. I also made a report in writing to the Archdeacon and Mr. Ward at the ensuing visitation of the state of the Chapel and negligence of Chapel Wardens and requested a particular admonition might be given them. But Mr. Ward thought little cognisance could be taken of the affair unless the Chapel Wardens were formally presented for neglect of duty. For may own part I believed a strict admonition would be sufficient and was unwilling singly to incur the odium of many individuals of the Townships by bringing them under the penalties and trouble of the Court and if your Lordship knew the temper and character of these people such reluctance would appear pardonable. At present the legality and propriety of the order in Vestry passed at Easter for raising 100£ by a Chapel Rate is no longer questioned. But my Chapel Wardens have recourse to procrastination. The Warden of Denton has taken some steps towards the collection, the Warden of Haughton has done nothing. They seem to be intimidated by the fear of opposition from a few turbulent payers and I suspect secretly cherish a wish to throw off the business upon their successors. But if your Lordship would be pleased merely to address a short admonitory letter to these Chapel Wardens and require them to proceed immediately in their duty I flatter myself that would answer all the purposes of a formal presentation. And now that your Lordship may not form a worse opinion of the inhabitants of these Townships than they really deserve it becomes my duty to say that there are many well disposed persons amongst them who wish to see the Chapel decently preserved. But the general sentiment is perhaps rather in favour of a new Chapel than of expending large sums in supporting the old one which can not possibly endure much longer.

"Of the population which is great and increasing, the present Chapel can scarcely contain one tenth part. There is no gallery excepting a small one for the Singers and the area of the ground floor is chiefly appropriated to the Tenantry and Estates of the Earl of Wilton, W. Hulton, Esq. of Hulton Park and G. H. Clarke, Esq. of Hyde in Cheshire. I have just reason for believing that my late noble and much to be lamented Patron was well inclined towards the re-building of the Chapel. As to Mr. Hulton I cannot flatter myself that he would contribute to such an undertaking having lately had occasion to address him on subjects of parochial Charity but without success. Mr. Clarke of Hyde attends divine service at Denton during Summer and spends the Winter in London. On the question of a new Chapel he is strenuously adverse but expresses great concern for keeping the ancient edifice in repair. Upon the whole I think our present circumstances and prospects unpropitious to a new Chapel.

"It only remains, my Lord, for me to renew with respectful deference my preceding request that your Lordship would be pleased to admonish the Chapel Wardens in order that a convenient and legal mode of providing for repairs may be speedily resorted to and the rites of the Chapel asserted whilst precedents of former Chapel rates are still extant and living witnesses ready to attest that such rates have the sanction of ancient and constant usage to a period within present recollection.

"I have the honour to remain with great respect,
My Lord,
Your Lordship's very
obedient Servant.
W.P.G.

"Denton, near Manchester.
29th November 1815."[1]

In Favour of a New Chapel

To what a low ebb things had come! Even Mr. Parr Greswell has to admit that the old Chapel "cannot possibly endure much longer." Worse still, it cannot serve the community as a whole because it "can scarcely contain one tenth part" of the population. Even if they had wanted to attend public worship on a Sunday they would have found most seats reserved for the families of those tenants who lived on the estates of the Earl of Wilton, Mr. W. Hulton and Mr. G. Hyde Clarke. Grieved though

[1] This letter has never been published before.

Mr. Parr Greswell was by the state of the Chapel it is possible he had been even more grieved by the building of Haughton Wesleyan Methodist Church[1] on Two Trees Lane five years earlier. He would consider it an affront to himself as Minister, to the Established Church and to King George III, the Head of that Church. But is it any wonder that so many became Methodists when the Church of England seemed to care so little for the Gospel and virtually turned people from her doors. Even as he wrote a *second* Wesleyan Church was being built on Ashton Road![2]

Many years later, (in 1836) Hope Congregational was built on Stockport Road. From the day of its erection to the day of his death Parr Greswell was never seen to walk past it without first crossing to the other side of the road.[3] Indeed, Denton had to wait until the 1880's before its Church of England clergy began to develop friendly relations with nonconformist ministers.

The crisis which had come to a head at Denton in 1815 had developed because of the irregularity in local affairs to which Mr. Parr Greswell refers in his second paragraph. For some years past those few chapel repairs which had been carried out had been paid for out of the poor rate. This sounds very bad, but we know that in Denton it did not lead to the neglect of the poor. In many parishes the church and poor rates were not always kept as completely separate accounts; the surplus of the church rate sometimes being added to the poor rate and vice versa. In 1784 there had been a Chapel rate and money from it was added to the poor rate, whilst in 1785 money from the poor rate was used to make up the amount needed by the Chapel Wardens for their repairs. But by 1815 the church tax (i.e. the district chapel rate) had not been collected for some years and the Overseers of the Poor were refusing to forward any more money to reimburse the Chapel Wardens. Even when Mr. Parr Greswell finally persuades the Vestry to levy £100 on the lay payers of Denton and Haughton the Wardens are afraid to collect it. No doubt they would meet with opposition not only from aggressive parishioners who did not like being taxed, some of whom would be non-conformists,[4] but also from those who objected to money being spent on a building that had had its day. "The general senti-

[1] 1810 is early for a Wesleyan Chapel and as the second oldest building for worship in Denton it should be highly prized.

[2] It was opened in 1816 and stood where we now find the Denton and Haughton Co-operative Society. In 1871 the congregation moved to Hyde Road, where they had built a larger church – the present Denton Methodist.

[3] Wainwright Manuscript.

[4] Non-Conformists deeply resented the Church Rate. Through it they were compelled to support a church which they did not attend and of which they did not approve. Gladstone's Government abolished the Rate in 1868, but it had been largely unenforceable in town parishes since the 1830's.

ment is perhaps rather in favour of a new Chapel than of expending large sums in supporting the old one which cannot possibly endure much longer." Here is one of the most important sentences in the letter. Most people thought that the old chapel should be pulled down and a bigger, better one erected, towards which they would have subscribed willingly. A study of the poor law records shows that Denton and Haughton were well administered villages in which paupers were cared for in a compassionate and generous manner. Two paid Overseers of the Poor saw to it that the poor were treated with consideration and common sense.[1] Parr Greswell calls them "indolent and contumacious," but their indolence consisted in their refusal to forward money for repairs because they considered it a waste of good money to go on repairing an edifice which could not possibly endure much longer!

One further point needs to be made before the situation can be fully understood. This was the first (and almost certainly the last) *District* Chapel Rate that Parr Greswell levied. When he arrived in 1791 he discovered that the custom had grown up of imposing a ley (that is a rate) upon "such freeholders and others as possess pews in the Chapel . . . each being obliged to pay in proportion to their number of seats."[2] In other words the congregation allowed themselves to be taxed in order to pay the cost of repairs. But in 1815 Parr Greswell was determined to raise the large sum of £100 and in order to do so he appeals to the ancient custom of taxing *all* freeholders in Denton and Haughton whether they held pews in the Chapel or not. This was why he had to use his authority (and that of the Bishop) to the utmost in order to persuade the vestry to agree with him and he was willing to risk a good deal of unpopularity in the process. In subsequent years they went back to the ley charged upon pewholders only and in 1836 even that was abolished. Voluntary subscriptions replaced levies.

Success at Last

But all was not lost! We know from a longhand note written inside the back cover of the baptism and funeral register for 1787–1812 that the appeal to the bishop must have had its desired effect. It reads:

"The Chapel was repaired both inside and out in the year 1816 and Denton side[3] pewed.

Gabriel Lupton, Chapelwarden of Denton
Robert Thornley, Chapelwarden for Haughton."

[1] See Mrs. Shirley Jarratt's exceedingly fine thesis "The Operation of the old Poor Law in Denton and Chorlton-cum-Hardy 1780–1800".
[2] Answers given by Parr Greswell to questions asked by the Governors of Queen Anne's Bounty, 1792.
[3] The North side. Haughton people sat on the South side.

What were these repairs exactly? Does any more detailed account of them exist? The answer to this question depends on what we make of a fascinating passage in the Revd. John Booker's famous work *A History of the Ancient Chapel of Denton*, published by the Chetham Society in 1855. Booker is a mine of information, and on pp. 45–46 gives an account of restoration which must be quoted in full. He says, however, that these extensive repairs took place in 1791 when Parr Greswell was appointed to the Incumbency. Yet three pages earlier (on p. 41) he makes passing reference to what seems to be the *same* restoration and dates it "about the year 1820". Moreover, he doesn't seem to have known of the note inside the back cover of the old register and this is probably the basic reason for his inconsistency,[1] Here, then, is Booker's account:

"When appointed to the incumbency in 1791, he found numerous skylights and other apertures in the roof caused by the wind displacing the slates, through which the rain and snow found access; and this to such an extent as to cause long strips of the ceiling to give way and to fall, to the serious interruption of the services and the discomfort of the minister and people. At this period, through age and decay, the walls of the edifice resembled a riddle. Mr. Greswell recommended the roof to be taken off and reslated, the horizontal ceiling to be removed[2] and the chapel left, as he conjectured it had originally been, open to the roof. He further suggested that the exterior should be cemented, and that internally upright beams should be placed against the old walls, that these should be filled with lath and plaster, the old walls being thus encased. The labour of restoration having been commenced, the vibration attendant on fixing the beams caused sundry coats of whitewash to start from the walls, when, to the astonishment of the workmen, several words in old English characters were discovered, and on further search, under the superintendence of Mr. Greswell, the whole history of Dives and Lazarus,[3] taken from an older version of the Scriptures than the authorised edition now in use, was discovered written upon the walls.[4] This inscription still remains, but, of course, concealed by the recent plaster to which the walls were subjected. Two heraldic shields, with the names of Hulton de Hulton

[1] He also failed to check the Chapel Warden's accounts. Fortunately, the accounts for 1787–1799 have survived at the back of a poor relief book, now in the care of the Librarian of Denton Public Library. Only small amounts were spent on running repairs; for example £1.11.9½d. in 1792 and £3.6.4½d. in 1799.

[2] This flat inner ceiling had been installed in 1726.

[3] Luke 16, verses 19–31.

[4] This older version could have been The Great Bible (1539) or "The Breeches Bible" (1560) or The Bishop's Bible (1568).

and Hyde de Denton were also at the same time discovered at the east end of the chapel on removing from the panel the coating of plaster, whereon in modern times the Decalogue had been inscribed."[1]

The astonishment of the workmen is understandable for they would suddenly catch a glimpse of what the Chapel walls must have looked like when Denton was a strong centre of Puritanism during the ministry of John Angier (1632–1677) and other seventeenth century divines. What other Bible stories were on the walls we shall never know. But one thing we do know: in 1816 Parr Greswell saved the old Chapel. Without him it would have perished.

---

[1] The Revd. J. Booker, M.A.: *A History of the Ancient Chapel of Denton* (Chetham Society, 1855), pp. 45–46.

CHAPTER TWO

GEORGE HYDE CLARKE 1742–1824

THE HYDES of Hyde were an important and well-connected English family. They were extremely wealthy and by the middle of the eighteenth century had become owners of large estates on both sides of the Atlantic. Hyde Hall, the family home, stood on the banks of the river Tame, opposite Glass House Fold, until it was demolished in 1857.

Edward Hyde went to America as Governor of North Carolina and as his son died without issue the name of Hyde was continued through his daughter Anne, who in 1714, married George Clarke, the Lieutenant Governor of New York. Their children – nine of them – were called Hyde Clarke.

One of these nine children, Edward, settled in Jamaica. He married a rich widow, Elizabeth, and owned six thousand acres of sugar plantation, worked by five hundred and seventy negro slaves.

George Hyde Clarke, born in 1742, was the son of Edward and Elizabeth. No doubt he enjoyed all the privileges that came naturally to a person in his position. He seems to have been as familiar with England as he was with Jamaica and in 1767 or thereabouts married Catherine, daughter of Robert Hussey of Denore in Ireland.

George Hyde Clarke. From an old painting.

Did he then set off on a Grand Tour of the capitals of Europe and Italy with his Irish wife? To go on the Grand Tour was certainly part of a young gentleman's education, but usually one went with a tutor. Something, however, – perhaps an extended honeymoon – took George to France, because we know that his eldest son – also called George – was born in Dijon on April 28th, 1768 and baptised there in St. John's Roman Catholic Church. Two years later, when they were staying in Lyons, a second son, Edward, was born on November 28th and he was baptized in St. Peter's Catholic Church.

In July 1772 the family returned home to Denton, where an extraordinary scene took place in the old chapel, presided over by the Curate,[1] Mr. William Jackson. The father of these two boys insisted on having them re-baptized. His strong protestant upbringing had made everything Roman Catholic repugnant to him and so on July 19th they all gathered round the font. George (4 years) and Edward (1 year 8 months) were re-baptized and then Hector, a negro servant, aged 14 years, was brought forward for baptism. He was undoubtedly a slave, very probably born in Jamaica, and Mr. Hyde Clarke was obliged to have him baptized because the Lord Chief Justice, Lord Mansfield, had ruled that as soon as a slave steps on to English soil he becomes a free man.[2] His baptism effectually made him a citizen of England. Poor boy! One wonders if he had any understanding of what was being done as he stood there to have the water sprinkled on his head in the name of the Trinity. No doubt he was wearing the ornate uniform or livery into which personal servants were put in order to give a touch of social cachet to the wealthy families of Georgian England.

A Good-Looking Girl

George Hyde Clarke was now thirty and a leading man in society. He seems to have divided his time between England and Jamaica and his movements are hard to trace accurately. He must, however, have spent enough time in Lancashire and Cheshire for strong passions to develop between himself and Sophia Astley, the Squire of Duninfield's daughter. She was a very good-looking girl and people said that she had been spoilt by her father.[3] Suddenly she disappeared. She had eloped to Jamaica with George who also took his wife Catherine and his two boys with him! There, Sophia gave birth to an illegitimate son on October 31st, 1777.

[1] Incumbents of Denton Chapel were called Curates. They were not called Rectors until 1854.
[2] This famous court decision 'The Mansfield Judgement' had been given just a month earlier, on June 22nd, 1772.
[3] T. Middleton: *History of Hyde* (1932), page 415.

On December 15th he was baptized Hyde John Clarke in the parish church of Trelawny in the County of Cornwall, Jamaica.[1]

The Mark of Ownership

It was in the same year, 1777 that George Hyde Clarke came into the sugar estates of Hyde and Swanswick which he inherited from his uncle, Edward Clarke. They consisted of one thousand acres and 220 negro slaves whom he had branded on the shoulder with the initials G.H.C. A silver brand was used because the wounds from silver were said to heal more quickly and not to fester. A replica of George Hyde Clarke's brand can be seen in the Wilberforce Museum, Hull.

George Hyde Clarke's Silver Slave Brand.
Courtesy of the Wilberforce Museum, Hull.

A Marriage is Arranged

Sophia was George's mistress for fifteen years. She bore him a second son, Robert Clarke, on March 5th, 1779 who was baptized in Denton Chapel on March 21st.[2] This shows us that the family was back in England but they returned to Jamaica again within two years.

Sophia's father, John Astley, had been a wild one in his youth, for whom things turned out very well. He entered into the estates of Dukinfield

[1] Parish Register of Trelawny, Jamaica. I am grateful to Mrs. Elizabeth Capstick, a historical research worker of Mandeville, Jamaica for this information.
[2] Parish Baptism register, page 37.

17

by a lucky marriage to a rich widow. Before that he was a successful portrait painter in London, one of the school of Sir Joshua Reynolds, with whom he had travelled in Italy. By now he was a respectable Squire and he felt hurt and enraged by his daughter's conduct, so when he came to make his will in 1786, he left her an annuity of £100, which was to cease "if she should at any time live or cohabit with that execrable villain, George Hyde Clarke of the island of Jamaica."[1]

He died the following year and Sophia must then have learned of the annuity, but she continued to live with George for another five years. It is said that he offered a Frenchman, Monsieur Lious Foncier,[2] £1,000 to marry her, which he obligingly did in St. Marylebone Church, London, on September 20th, 1792.[3] They lived together at Wem in Shropshire and Sophia bore her husband a son and a daughter. Reaching the age of 82 she died on November 7th, 1831 and is buried at Wem.

Upholding the Injustice of Slavery

In 1781 George had been made a vestryman in the parish of Trelawny and in 1785 a Justice of the Peace and Assistant Judge in the Court of Common Pleas.[4] This meant that he played a very real part in upholding the status quo in the West Indies and it is worth reminding ourselves of its nature.

We have no means of telling whether George was a brutal or humane slave-holder, but we do know that the average life expectancy of a negro slave was only seven years. They lived in hovels and were worked extremely hard. Sometimes they tried to run away and notices appeared in newspapers listing them. George's slaves were no exception. The *Royal Gazette* carried these two notices referring to slaves who had been caught on the run and taken to local workhouses to await collection:

"In St. Ann's Workhouse, December 30th 1795
　　　Charles – to George H. Clarke – a Creole 5′ 6″
In Trelawny Workhouse, Jan. 25th 1796
　　　Putney – to Hyde Estate – an Eboe, no visible marks.
　　　Jacob – to Hyde Estate – no visible marks."[5]

[1] T. Middleton: *History of Hyde* (1932), pages 415–416.
[2] Middleton gives the name as Foucier, but it was in fact Foncier.
[3] Boyd's marriage Index for Middlesex. In 1771, Richard Cumberland's comedy, "The West Indian" was performed at The Theatre Royal, Drury Lane. The title refers to an English slave-holder who has just returned from the West Indies. (In the 18th Century what we now call West Indians were called negroes). On arriving in London, the first thing he does is to try to acquire a mistress! George Hyde Clarke's conduct with Sophia was not all that unusual.
[4] Official and other personages of Jamaica by W. A. Feurtado.
[5] *The Royal Gazette* 1795–6. I am grateful to Mrs. Elizabeth Capstick for this information.

Punishment for slaves was often sadistic. At St. Ann's Bay Slave Court three men had their ears and noses cut off and received thirty-nine lashes every Sunday for three weeks.

"In St. Thomas in the East, in 1783, a slave named Mercury was found with ten pounds of fresh veal in his possession. No proof is given that he came dishonestly by it, but he had his right ear cut off; fifty lashes were inflicted at the same time, and he received fifty lashes more twice a month for six months, and during that period was worked in chains. Two women ran away: they were branded on both cheeks, and received thirty-nine lashes once a week for a month, and worked in chains. But poor Priscilla fared far worse in 1783 and 1784. She too had made an effort to escape. Both ears were cut off. She was placed in chains, and sentenced to receive thirty-nine lashes on the first Monday in each month for a whole year."[1]

Was George troubled in his conscience over slavery? We shall never know. Probably he believed, as did so many prosperous people, that if slavery were abolished, England's economy would be ruined. So he contented himself with giving a piece of land from his Swanswick estate on which St. Michael's church was built in the middle of the little village called Clarke's Town. It was one of a number of small churches in that part of the island and they were all packed each Sunday with congregations of slaves.[2]

The Respected Patron

In 1798–9 the Hyde Clarke family returned to Hyde Hall on the banks of the Tame. This was their summer residence; in winter they lived in London, on Grafton Street, Berkeley Square. George had been made Commissioner of the Peace for Cheshire in 1772. The authorities must have regarded him as a very valuable man as far as law and order were concerned so in 1790 he was made a Justice of the Peace for Lancashire, enabling him to act in the name of the King on both sides of the Tame. Having permanently settled in England, he became a "constant attendant at Denton Chapel" during the summer and was certainly the most important member of Mr. Parr Greswell's congregation. As we have seen, his liberal contributions towards the repairs helped to save the chapel from collapse.

When he attended Divine Service did Mr. Parr Greswell's sermons offend him? Certainly not! As we shall see, Parr Greswell seems to have had little or no social conscience and is highly unlikely to have campaigned

---

[1] W. J. Gardner: *History of Jamaica* (1909), page 178.
[2] Dan Ogilvie: *History of the Parish of Trelawny.*

against the slave trade or to have supported William Wilberforce. Denton Chapel should have been a place where a congregation of Christian people gathered who longed to establish justice, freedom and compassion in the world. Unfortunately, like to many other churches, they were mostly the privileged of society who cared more about pride of wealth and class than they did about Christ and his teaching. They expected the clergy to support their political views, to maintain an extravagant courtesy towards them and to use their influence to keep the lower orders content with their lot. But this was not easy – sedition was in the air.

"Twisting-In"

As the Industrial Revolution progressed, Britain became more and more dependent on selling manufactured goods abroad. All was well when markets were open, but in 1811 the United States closed the American markets to British Goods and as the European markets were already closed by the Napoleonic wars, a very serious situation arose.[1] All over the country factories stood idle and working people faced starvation. Employers, at their wits' end to keep going, not only reduced wages, but speeded up the new machinery which enabled the cheap labour of children to be substituted for that of adults. Riots broke out. Frame-breaking began and from 1811–1816 Luddites caused endless trouble.

They got their name from a character called "General Ludd" who was supposed to be their leader. There was no such person. Nevertheless, they were to some extent organised and everyone joining the movement had to swear a secret oath of loyalty to his fellows. This was known as "twisting-in" and magistrates such as George Hyde Clarke, were extremely worried by the number of Luddites in Hyde and its neighbourhood. Gangs of them blacked their faces, armed themselves with clubs and attacked factories to break machines and shops to steal food.

In July 1811, five troops of Scots Greys arrived at Manchester to help keep the peace and within a year the Duke of Montrose's Light Dragoons were ordered from Kent to Ashton-under-Lyne. One of their captains was Francis Raynes, who published an account of his adventures in 1817. With help from the local population he was successful in making a number of arrests – one of the most important being that of James Haigh of Dukinfield, a noted ringleader, on August 26th, 1812.

To help the soldiers, Mr. George Hyde Clarke and his fellow magistrates swore in a number of good rate-payers as special constables and by frequent letters they kept each other abreast of events:

[1] Middleton: *History of Hyde* (1932), page 68.

20

Hyde, 28th August, 1812.

"Mr. Hyde Clarke's compliments to Captain Raines, that he has sworn in the oath of allegiance to 95 men, but there will be with him to-morrow he believes 50 or more. H. C. has had a great deal of his business to attend to yesterday and to-day, so put them off until to-morrow. James Smith of Dukinfield, weaver, was sworn in by James Haigh, as also John Spragg at the same time. John Spragg, weaver in Dukinfield, *Twisted in* three months ago, by James Haigh. James Smith works with John Spragg and *twisted in* at the same time Spragg was, by James Haigh. I can see only the two above that James Haigh has *twisted in*. Spragg works for William Taylor of Ashton. I believe this James Haigh is a great rogue. Excuse haste. H. C. will be in Stockport on Monday."[1]

Mr. Hyde Clarke had obviously taken confessions from James Smith and John Spragg who had been brought before him. The very next day William Moss, a cotton spinner of Dukinfield was brought before him and he too confessed that he had been twisted in by James Haigh.[2] Great would be Mr. Hyde Clarke's delight when he heard of Haigh's arrest. After an appearance before him in Stockport, he was committed for trial at Chester.

The Attack on the Corn Mill

Five months earlier a gang of men had attacked Arden corn mill on the Bredbury bank of the Tame. Masonry from this mill can still be seen in the river from the path through Denton woods below the cemetery.[3] These "Luddites" were all after flour. They intimidated Joseph Clay, the miller, seized the mill and sold off flour cheaply to the surrounding population. The Scots Greys were brought out and four arrests were made – Samuel Lees, 32 years, James Ratcliffe, 22 years, Thomas Etchells, 34 years, (all hatters of Denton) and Thomas Burgess, 35 years, a collier of Bredbury. A fifth man, however, got away. This was Nathan Howard. The soldiers shot at him as he leapt over the mill dam, but he escaped – and emigrated.

After appearing before the Magistrates at Stockport (and possibly before Mr. Hyde Clarke himself), they were committed for trial at Chester with eighteen others who had been rounded up at places such as Bolton, Wilms-

[1] Quoted by Middleton from Raynes: *History of Hyde* (1936), page 71.
[2] Raynes: *Appeal to the Public*, pages 90–91.
[3] Later it became a paper mill and the turbines are still in position. It must be approached down the long cobbled road by the Arden Arms. It is a dangerous and exciting site, crying out for study by students of industrial archaeology.

low, Hyde and Congleton. It was not the normal Assize but a Special Commission in the castle before Judges R. Dallas, F. Burton and a jury on May 27th. Before proceedings began, Judge Dallas delivered an impressive speech:

"Gentlemen of the Jury –

It is not my practice to trespass upon your time with any desultory observations; indeed, the general state of the Calendar seldom requires any particular remarks. The present instance, however, is one of an unusual nature – of a more complicated aspect in respect to guilt. It is not necessary for me to refer you to the scenes which have lately taken place amongst you. We now sit here under a Special Commission, which his R.H. the Prince Regent, acting in the name and on the behalf of his Majesty, has been pleased to appoint, to investigate those disgraceful proceedings which have so long agitated the manufacturing districts of this and the neighbouring counties, and which demand a necessary and early example. The number of commitments for riots, which guilt ramifies into every possible shape and form, is unprecedented and alarming. Taken by itself, the act of riot classes but as a misdemeanour, to which the variations of specific offence have attached different degrees of punishment. The Offence of taking and administering an unlawful oath or engagement, the Legislature has made capital; it comes in the shape of a felony, and both are put on the same footing as to punishment. With respect to the purport of an unlawful oath, I shall refer you to the statutes. It is not necessary the express words of an engagement of this nature should be mentioned in an indictment. The act of taking the oath constitutes the crime; and even the person who, by compulsatory measures, assents to such a covenant, is held a participator in the crime, unless he makes a declaration thereof to a Magistrate within four days from the period when he assented to its purport. But Gentlemen, if on legal points you shoult find yourselves at a loss, I have to request you will refer to the Court, from whom you will receive the information required. Several charges, under the description of robbery will come under your cognizance; and here, Gentlemen, it may be necessary to put you in possession of the construction the law has put upon the word: An act of robbery must be proved to have been by force, or by putting in fear; and the investigation of these points will be essentially necessary in the present special inquiry; but on this head no difficulty is likely to occur. It is not necessary, to constitute a robbery, that actual personal violence should be used; expressions or threatening attitudes are equally within the meaning of the word. During the riots in London, in the year 1780, a boy with a cockade in his hat knocked at a trades-man's door, and when it was opened, he accosted him – "God bless your honour, remember the poor mob." The tradesman rebuked the boy, and turned him out, when the boy said he would go back and fetch their captain, meaning one of the leaders of the mob; which he did, and the gentleman gave him half-a-crown. This was accounted robbery, the money being given under the influence of fear, which the Court held to be as decisive as if personal violence had been offered. In obedience to what I feel my duty, and with these allusions to what the law is, I shall bring my observations to a conclusion, always relying, as I now do on the discrimination, caution and praise-worthy conduct of a Cheshire Jury. I have performed my judicial duty, and I do not think it prudent or proper to proceed any further. On the general feature of the cases for your consideration, I have no reason to form any very pleasing conjectures. Distress, I fear, did not operate as some would wish us to believe. The characteristics of the system of disturbance are of a very different colour. Handbills were printed and circulated in the manufacturing districts, holding out hopes to the disaffected, and threats to the well-disposed. A secret oath was administered – the crest and consolidation of conspiracy – all these denote the intrigues of wicked and designing men, to create riot and partial injury. Justice has been for a while withheld, but the law must now unfold its terrors, always remembering, as we shall, that confi-dence and consideration so necessary in its execution."[1]

The trial then began and all but two were convicted. The four who attacked Arden corn mill were sentenced to seven years transportation and a fine of one shilling each. They were luckier than eight rioters convicted at a Special Assize at Lancaster a fortnight later. They were all hanged and one of them was a woman who had been caught stealing potatoes![2] Samuel Lees and James Radcliffe had both been baptized in Denton Chapel. All four were married and Burgess was the only one without children. Of the children only Samuel Lees' appear in Denton Chapel register, but there were five and Parr Greswell had baptized them all. How terrible it must have been for his wife Anne to be left "to the parish" with Samuel, 10 years, Joseph, 8 years, Nancy, 5 years, Benjamin, 3 years and Mary only 4 months.

[1] *The Gentleman's Magazine*, June 1812, page 583.
[2] Ibid., page 583.

At the end of June the prisoners were taken by coach from Chester Castle to Woolwich and handed over to the master of Retribution Hulk.[1] From there we can trace them no further. Were they sent to Botany Bay? Did they survive? There are no more records of them. They disappear into history.

But what of James Haigh – the Twister-in? Inexplicably, he got off! Captain Raynes and Mr. Hyde Clarke were very annoyed about it, but justice is never quite as even-handed as all that.

By now Mr. George Hyde Clarke was seventy. The remaining twelve years of his life were very comfortable. He died in London on July 5th, 1824 and his body was drawn in solemn procession all the way to Denton, passing through Stockport on July 15th[2] to be laid to rest in Denton Chapel-yard the next day. No doubt, in his sermon, Mr. Parr Greswell spoke highly of him, as does the inscription on the gravestone preserved on the Market Street side. Its bold letters pay tribute to a respected patron and bring a chapter in the life of our parish to a close.

"GEORGE HYDE CLARKE

Late of Hyde
in the County of Chester
Esquire
during his life-time
a constant Attendant
at this Chapel
and
a Liberal Contributor
to its Repairs
Died in London

June V[3] MDCCCXXIV

aged LXXXII Years
and agreeably to
his own special directions
was here interred
on the XVI July
following."

Six years later, in March 1830, his long-suffering wife Catherine died at Bath.

[1] Trial Records, Cheshire Record Office.
[2] *Stockport Advertiser*, July 16th, 1824.
[3] The stone mason has made a mistake. It should read July V.

CHAPTER THREE

WILLIAM PARR GRESWELL, 1765–1854

IN 1791, the people of Denton and Haughton must have been pleased to hear that their new Curate intended to come and live in the parish. His predecessor, Mr. William Jackson, had not done so. He was master of Stockport Grammar School and rode over to Denton on Sundays and on those other days when his services were required. Furthermore, the old Parsonage (known as 'The Chapelhouse'), which stood at the north-east corner of the chapelyeard, had been let as an ale-house for many years, the money augmenting the Minister's salary but depriving him of a place to live. Parr Greswell was not satisfied with such a state of affairs so the Earl of Wilton agreed to build him a house. As it was not ready until about 1794, the Curate rode over from Blackley, a journey of seven to eight miles.[1]

Wilton House, The Parsonage,
photograph by David Walker.

[1] Samuel Hadfield: *"A Historical Glance at Denton Chapel"*, a newspaper article in the *Ashton Standard*, September 27th, 1862.

When finished, the new parsonage was excellent.[1] It stands on the left hand side of Ashton Road as you go towards Guide Bridge, almost opposite the end of Greswell Street which, of course, was named after him many years later. In those days (the end of the eighteenth century) farmland stretched on either side of Ashton Road and Parr Greswell's spacious home had a garden and two pastures.

The Little Grammar School

As the living of Denton was very poor – only £100 per year – Mr. Parr Greswell opened a Grammar School in his home to teach his own sons and those of well-to-do people in the neighbourhood. Being a classical scholar he was in his element teaching them Latin and Greek, essential if they were to enter any profession. His astonishing success in sending five of his own seven sons to Oxford is well known[2] and he must have been an excellent teacher for no less a person than William Roscoe of Liverpool sent two of his wards of court, William and Dobson Lowndes, to be educated by him. Thomas Isherwood of Marple Hall also attended the school. He was the great-grandfather of Christopher Isherwood, the famous twentieth century novelist.

John and Joseph Sidebotham were two more pupils. Joseph became the first person to take photographs in Denton and to him we owe the precious picture of Parr Greswell taken in 1853, less than a year before his death. To his brother John we are indebted for a little story which gives a glimpse of life at the school. "He used to send me out to Quebec pit to get a willow cane." "Well!" said his friend, "but I should not have liked such a job if I had been in your place, Mr. John." "Oh! I didn't mind it, for I knew what sort to get."[3]

The 1848 Ordnance Survey map shows that there was a Quebec Farm[4] about one hundred yards up Ashton Road opposite Wilton House and in a field behind it was a coalpit. It was one of those many little mines which farmers opened up as a side-line and worked in the winter months. By the pit were two ponds and no doubt willow trees grew there. Parr Greswell would give the boy a knife with which to cut a cane. When he returned he would be required to kneel on a chair and Mr. Greswell would cane him on the "posterior" – to use what he would consider the correct word.

[1] After Parr Greswell's death it was divided into a pair of semi-detached houses called Wilton Villas. Today it is the surgery of Doctors P. Brodbin and C. A. O'Conner.
[2] Middleton: *History of Denton and Haughton* (Hyde 1936), page 67. We must not over-estimate the achievement. Oxford was closed to all except Church of England boys until Glasdtone's Government opened it to all males in 1871.
[3] Joel Wainwright: *Memoirs of Marple* 1899, page 47.
[4] Quebec Street now stands on this land.

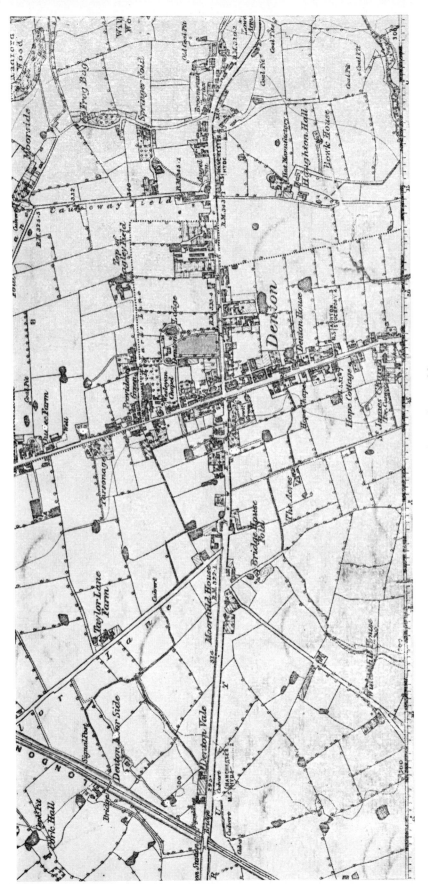

From the 1848 Ordnance Survey Map.

A Poor Living Augmented

Parr Greswell did not receive tithes. These were paid to Manchester Parish Church. Where then did his stipend come from? Mostly from invested monies given over the years, but the amounts were so small that in 1791 the Living was only yielding an income of £60 per annum![1] It was raised as follows:—

Interest from £600 invested through the Governors of
Queen Anne's Bounty .. .. £12. 0.0.
Rent from the Chapelhouse .. .. £16.16.0.
Income from Pew Rents .. .. £23. 0.0.
Surplice Fees (Approx.) .. .. £3. 0.0.
Interest on £175 invested with Jones's Bank, Manchester £6. 2.6.
———
£60.18.6.

The Chapelhouse, the old parsonage, let as an Ale-House

The Bishop of Chester, the Earl of Wilton and the Governors of Queen Anne's Bounty were all concerned about this shocking state of affairs. No wonder Mr. Jackson had not lived in the parish. It was too poor to support an Incumbent. Something had to be done and over the next nine years successful efforts were made to raise the Living to £100. After the

[1] The details which follow are taken from correspondence now in the Lancashire Record Office.

Governors of Queen Anne's Bounty had given £400 and the Earl £200, an estate was bought in Haughton which could be let for £30 per year. (It was purchased from John Wagstaffe and consisted of a dwellinghouse, a barn, a shippen and a warehouse, eight fields, a small orchard and a garden; all fenced. The tenant was James Ashworth, an awkward man, who had only paid Wagstaffe £21 per year and had to be evicted).

In 1800 the Jack Heyes estate was bought from Robert Thornley. This was also in Haughton and consisted of 6½ Lancashire acres. It was let for about £18 per year and the position at the turn of the century was as follows:—

Rent from Wagstaffe's Estate	.. ..	£30. 0.0.
„ „ Jack Heyes Estate	.. .. .. about	£18. 0.0.
„ „ The Chapelhouse	.. ..	£16.16.0.
Income from Pew Rents	.. ..	£23. 0.0.
Surplice Fees ..	.. ..at least	£3. 0.0.
Interest from £200 invested with Jones's Bank	.. ..	£6.17.6.
		————
		£97.13.6.

Because the Living of Denton was worth so little the idea has persisted to this day that Parr Greswell remained a poor man all his life, but this popular myth fails to take account of the substantial fees paid to him for educating the sons of gentry and the fact that he lived in a rent free house. He also inherited real estate from relatives and his will (published in Appendix I) shows that by the time he died he owned houses in Salford, Strangeways, Saddleworth in the West Riding of Yorkshire – and nine cottages at Crown Point! This alters the picture so dramatically that we are not surprised to find him spending large sums on books. He could afford to be a "reading parson".

The Earl of Wilton allowed James Ashworth, (the tenant who was evicted from Wagstaffe's estate in 1795) to rent land from him on the left-hand side of Ashton Road as one travels to Guide Bridge, next to the plot of land on which Wilton House was built! Parr Greswell had found that in addition to his house and garden, (for which he paid no rent) he needed more land, (perhaps for horses and a cow or two), so Ashworth sub-let a little close and meadow to him. All went well until 1804, when Ashworth gave Parr Greswell notice of the fact that he intended to raise his rent for the land *and* to charge him a quit rent for the Parsonage and part of the garden! Amazed by such a demand Parr Greswell wrote to the Earl, humbly requesting that the house and garden may be exempted from any right Ashworth may claim upon them.

"My Lord,

"Mr. Ashworth, being according to report about to renew his lease of the estate he now occupies under your Lordship, I beg leave humbly to solicit that the house and premises at present, by your Lordship's kindness, in my possessions, may by a particular clause be exempted from any right or property he now claims in them – that for the little close consisting of about one cheshire acre which I hold – and from a very poor field have made into meadow at considerable expense, I may, when practicable, have the honour to become tenant to your Lordship and that the necessary liberty may be secured to myself or succeeding curates of inspecting and when requisite of opening the drain which passes through and discharges into Mr. Ashworth's fields. My apology for this request is that Mr. A. has made certain alterations in the open gutter by which the water is conveyed through a slack or hollow in your Lordship's land to the place where the field terminates – whence I am apprehensive of the covered drain being in a little time closed up, and the water thrown back upon the house. He has also lately given me notice that he not only intends to raise my rent for the field, but also expects I shall pay him a quit rent for part of the garden and premises – a demand never before made. As I attribute these circumstances to an unfriendly disposition, upon the part of James Ashworth, whom I am unconscious of having given any just cause of offence – your Lordship will naturally ask what can have interrupted the peace that ought to subsist between us. Hence it is proper I should state, in my own vindication that he happened some years ago to be the tenant upon the first estate purchased for the chapel – in my negotiations for which, from unjustifiable motives he sought, by many ways to impede and disappoint me. Amongst other attempts – a letter was clandestinely written (by whom or at whose instance I have little reason to doubt) tending to dishonour me and the Commissioners concerned with me in the opinion of the Governors of Queen Anne's Bounty – with how little of fact the inclosed correspondence, which took place on that occasion, will shew. Mr. Ashworth's obstinancy, at last obliged the vendor of the estate to eject him from the premises, before I could obtain possession. Mr. A. has ever since that transaction shown an unfriendly disposition towards me – and to this cause I attribute his recent conduct. Hence I cannot help wishing to have as little dependance upon or connection with him as possible. At the same time – my Lord, an earnest desire to preserve my own character inviolate in your Lordship's opinion occasions me to be thus particular in accounting for Mr. Ashworth's ill will. A consciousness of the obligations that lies upon us to return good for evil has hitherto, and would still have prevented me from laying these circumstances before your Lordship, had I not greatly feared a neglect of this timely application might subject me to further inconveniences. These being obviated it is my sincere hope and humble petition that nothing herein mentioned may operate to prejudice Mr. Ashworth's success in his present view of obtaining the continuance of your Lordship's favour as a tenant. By preventing in future any necessary connection between us, your Lordship will effectually shield me from any molestation on his part and I am sure, my own natural love of peace will preclude me from any voluntary altercation with him.

"William Cooke has lately made additions and improvements to the old Chapel house to the amount I believe, of one hundred pounds – and the purchase of the Chapel Land tax has been confirmed.

"I have the honour to remain
    with greatest respect,
    My Lord – Your Lordship's obliged and obedient
      Servant

        William Parr Greswell."

The request was granted. The Earl protected him from his annoying neighbour and when the Tithe Map of 1844[1] was drawn we find him enjoying the benefit of two pastures called New Meadow and Big Field.

The Sunday School and Day School
Most of the children of Denton belonged to the labouring classes and worked each day on farms and in factories. Their only schooling was on Sundays when they attended to learn reading, writing and arithmetic as well as Scripture, but many of them must have felt extremely tired. It was not until 1847 that an Act of Parliament reduced the hours children worked in mills to ten each day! The building, erected in 1769 stood to the left of the present lych gate as you face the church. Part of the land on which it stood is now graveyard, the rest is parking space. An inscribed stone records the fact that it was rebuilt by public subscription in 1814 and it remained in use until 1854, when St. Lawrence's School, Stockport Road, was opened.

[1] Lancashire Record Office.

Denton Old Church and School,
painted from a photograph by Mr. A. Wych.
By courtesy of Miss A. Wych.

The schoolmaster[1] lived in a house next to the school and taught those children whose parents could afford to send them on weekdays. At first this would be a very small number. Gradually as the years went by it would grow, but even as late as 1853 we know that only 66 boys and 40 girls enjoyed daily schooling.[2] On Sundays, however, 185 boys and 181 girls attended and the Sunday School Committee paid only three teachers half-a-crown per Sunday each to instruct them. They must have had their hands full!

It is remarkable that a school had been built as early as 1769. Not many parishes could boast a school open to children of the general public until much later on in the eighteenth century or even well on in the nineteenth! Denton's was built by voluntary subscriptions collected in the locality and there were twelve trustees, six for Denton, six for Haughton.

[1] The Chapel Warden's accounts for 1789 carry the following entry: "Paid for chusing and advertising for a schoolmaster 16 shillings."
[2] Middleton: *History of Denton and Haughton* (Hyde 1936), page 57.

We must not, however, assume that no education whatsoever was available before this date. Mr. John Lees of Town Lane (1705–1786) was practicing as a schoolmaster in 1740. We know this from a curious double-entry in the baptism registers of Denton and Gorton. The Denton register reads:—

The Gorton Register reads:—

> "Mary d. of John Lees of Townlene of Denton
> 22 May . . . . . 5 June 1740"

> "Mary d. of Mr. John Lees of Denton
> Schoolmaster . . . . . 5 June 1740."

Did he have her baptized twice on the same day? It's very unlikely, but what is of interest is the word "Schoolmaster". Was he Schoolmaster in Gorton? He might have been, but it is much more probable that he was a Schoolmaster in Denton for a Mr. Joseph Shaw had been appointed School-master at Gorton, only two years earlier.[1]

On March 2nd, 1742–3 John Lees was appointed Clerk at Denton Chapel. The word 'clerk' means someone who can read and write and his duties included writing the entries in the parish registers. He also had to attend church and lead the congregation in singing 'Amen' at the end of the prayers. He continued to be Clerk for twenty-two years with a short break from June 12th to October 23rd, 1763, finally relinquishing the office on August 17th, 1765.[2] He was sixty, but might have still been fit enough to carry on, but for some reason Mr. Jackson was dissatisfied. He appointed John Hyde of Haughton to be Clerk on August 23rd, 1765.[3]

Had this anything to do with the proposed school? Were people saying that the rough and ready way in which Mr. Lees taught the village boys to read and write wasn't good enough and that what they needed was a proper school? John Lees would hold his classes either in his own home or in the chapel itself and by 1765 the idea of building a school would be in the air. The document telling who the twelve trustees were has disappeared and we do not know if John Lees was one of them or not. Very probably not, but he continued to be an important member of the community and his will (published in Appendix II) makes interesting reading.

Middleton says that we don't know who the early schoolmasters were. The first we can name was Samuel Ashworth, who was master for a short time before going to Chadkirk school about 1815. "He was succeeded by Thomas Hyde Beeley, a noted local scholar and musician. Mr. Beeley

[1] *The Gorton Historical Recorder*, page 88.
[2] Note on fly-leaf of Parish Register 1724–1757.
[3] Note on fly-leaf of Parish Register 1758–1787.

remained master until his death in 1834 and was succeeded by his son, John Hyde Beeley, also a noted musician. In 1837 the last-named resigned[1] and was followed by John Pollitt, a pupil of the elder Beeley, who remained master until his death in October, 1854," aged fifty.[2] He had also been clerk of the chapel for nine years.[3]

"Sermons"

As Sunday School was free it was necessary to raise money. The accounts show that a lot was spent on pens, ink and copy books in which children learned to write texts and proverbs. They also bought candles and sconces (candle-holders), catechisms and Christmas pieces (carols). But heavier expenses were repairs, whitewashing the school, coal and, of course, the staff's quarterly salaries. So each year there was a "Sermons Sunday" when a special effort was made to collect enough to keep the Sunday School open. Handbills (such as the one reproduced on page 35) were posted up all over the town and a large congregation was expected. Notice that in 1829 the children themselves did not sing. They were probably not even present! Special adult performers who sang in the florid style of a Handel Oratorio were engaged to impress the congregation. And notice too that a real attempt is being made to keep the poor away. "N.B. SILVER WILL BE EXPECTED AT THE DOORS." Then, in the right hand column in block capitals we read "AFTER THE COLL-ECTION." Money was the very necessary end product of this exercise and the sermon would be devoted to the need for it. It was not until after the Education Act of 1870 that such begging sermons began to disappear. Gradually, as elementary education became universal, children ceased to be taught to read and write in Sunday School. So 'Sermons Sunday' changed its character and became the kind of Sunday School anniversary we know today.

'Sermons' was held on Trinity Sunday and Middleton records the story of what happened in 1843. The special preacher was the Revd. Hugh Stowell, Rector of Christ Church, Salford, but at the last moment he was prevented from attending so the church officers "postponed Trinity Sunday until the following week!"[4] On such occasions musicians from villages all around crammed into the gallery to provide music in addition to that of the little organ. Some of these performers played for over fifty years at the annual festival.

[1] Possibly because of ill health. He died in December, 1839, aged only 29.
[2] T. Middleton: page 57.
[3] Note in Burial Register, 1854.
[4] Middleton, page 130, column 2.   *Sermons Sunday Handbill.*

Selection of Sacred Music

TO BE PERFORMED IN

DENTON CHAPEL,

On SUNDAY the 14th. day of JUNE, 1829,

WHEN

A SERMON

WILL BE PREACHED BY THE

REV. J. HANDFORTH, MINISTER OF ST. MICHAEL'S CHURCH,

Ashton-under-Lyne,

And a Collection made towards the support of the Sunday School.

SERVICE TO BEGIN AT THREE O'CLOCK IN THE AFTERNOON.

N.B.—SILVER WILL BE EXPECTED AT THE DOORS.

LEADER MR. BARNES.

OPENING OF THE SERVICE.

MARTIN LUTHER'S HYMN.

GREAT God, what do I see and hear,
The ends of things created,
The judge of mankind doth appear
On clouds of glory seated :
The trumpet sounds, the graves restore
The dead which they contained before!

QUARTETTO.

When the ear heard him, then it blessed him ; and when the eye saw him, it gave witness of him.

CHORUS.

He delivered the poor that cried, the fatherless, and him that had none to help him. Kindness, meekness, and comfort were in his tongue. If there was any virtue, or of there was any praise, he thought on those things.

ANTHEM PLACE

AIR—*Mr. Grimshaw*

Why do the nations to furiously rage together, why do the people imagine a vain thing? the kings of the earth rise up, and the rulers take counsels together again the Lord and his anointed.

AIR—*Mr. Turner.*

I will be their God, and they shall be my people and the heathen shall know that I the Lord do sanctify Israel; when my sanctuary shall be in the midst of them

CHORUS—JOSHUA.

Ye sons of Israel, ev'ry tribe attend,
Let grateful songs and hymns to heav'n ascend ;
In Gilgal, and on Jordan's banks, proclaim
One fist, one great, one Lord Jehovah's hand

BEFORE THE SERMON.

AIR—*Mrs. Carrington*

HOLY, holy, Lord God Almighty, who was and is and is to come. Who shall not glorify thy name, for thou only art holy, thou only art the Lord.

DUET—*Messrs. Turner Grimshaw.*

Here shall soft charity repair
And break the bonds of grief ;
Smooth the furrow'd couch of care,
Man to man must bring relief.

AFTER THE COLLECTION

RECIT.—*Mr. Grimshaw* JUDETH

NE'ER doubt the mercy of the power divine,
But to the Lord bow down in humble pray'r :
Goodness and love does in his glory shine,
And to the faithful he will lend an ear :
Then, then your foes will backward flee
And from them all he'll set you free

AIR.

Conquest is not to bestow,
In the spear or in the bow ;
Nor does victory belong
To the valiant or the strong
But the pious and the just,
Those who in Jehovah trust ;
To their foes the sword shall give,
They shall triumph, they shall live

SONG—*Mrs. Carrington,*

O magnify the Lord, and worship him upon his holy hill, for the Lord our God is holy.

CHORUS—(MASS 7)—MOZART.

Glory be to God in the highest, and on earth peace, good will to men. We praise thee, and we bless thee, we adore thee, we glorify thee, we give thanks for thy great glory. O Lord God our heavenly King! God the Father Almighty! Glory be to God, and on earth peace, good will to men. Glory to God in the highest!—AMEN.

CUNNINGHAM, PRINTER, ASHTON-UNDER-LYNE.

From the Sunday School Treasurer's account book it is easy to see why the church officers were so anxious not to miss the collection in 1843. They had just spent £8.14.1d. giving the school a re-fitting throughout and although there were quarterly collections in chapel towards expenses, they were hoping for a particularly large one at "Sermons" that year. And they were not disappointed. Mr. Stowell's sermon drew £23.15.2½d. from the congregation.

Sunday Services

Parr Greswell was a conscientious parish priest, holding two services each Sunday. The first (which would begin about 10.30 a.m.) was known as "the full service." It consisted of Ante-communion,[1] Mattins and Litany, followed by a sermon and would last a good hour and a half. The order followed was that of the 1662 Prayer Book and all the psalms of the day would be sung. The sermon, which might last half an hour, was very probably read like an essay, carefully avoiding emotional overtones. Mr. Greswell would regard a 'Methodist' style of preaching as a vulgar attack on the emotions of the congregation and he would strongly disapprove of those Evangelical ministers within the Church of England who preached in this way. It is possible that on occasions he read the printed sermons of bishops and scholars to edify his hearers.

Until the 1840's services were always held within the hours of daylight, so Evensong would be said at about three or 3.30 p.m. Many parishes only had one service on Sunday but – thanks to an important letter – we know that Denton Chapel had two. This information comes to us from James Ralston, who, writing to Joel Wainwright in the third person as a mark of respect, looks back over the years and says:— "When he resided at Reddish Mill, and Denton Chapel being the nearest place of worship, he frequently attended the afternoon service there; more frequently perhaps on account of having read in the *Monthly Review* for October 1801 a very favourable criticism on Memoirs of and Translations from certain Italian writers of the 15th and 16th centuries by the Revd. Parr Greswell, Minister of the said Chapel . . . and was proud of having the privilege of seeing and hearing such a gentleman."[2]

Parr Greswell's fame as a scholar was already beginning to spread! But not everyone would be as impressed as Mr. Ralston. Perhaps Robert

[1] "Ante-communium" means the first part of the Holy Communion Service up to and including the Prayer for the Church Militant.

[2] This letter is so charming that it is printed in full in Appendix III of this book. Parr Greswell's answer to questions sent to him by the Governor's of Queen Anne's Bounty suggest that there had been two services each Sunday before 1791.

Booth found the service and sermon rather boring. He was put in the stocks one Sunday afternoon about the year of Nelson's death at Trafalgar (1805) for being drunk and causing a disturbance during the service. School children brought straw for him to lie on in case he had to remain out all night.[1]

Holy Communion would be administered ten or twelve times a year, possibly on a fixed Sunday of the month. This practice continued right up to the death of the Revd. David Rowe in 1915. The Revd. R. H. Bailey was the first Rector to introduce an early, weekly Communion.

Two special services are worth mentioning: "A Commination or denouncing of God's anger and judgements against Sinners," which was read each Ash Wednesday and "A Form of Prayer for the Fifth Day of November," being a thanksgiving for the deliverance of King James I and the three Estates of the Realm from gunpowder treason. "We yield Thee our unfeigned thanks and praise," Parr Greswell would pray, "for the wonderful and mighty deliverance of our gracious Sovereign King James the First, the Queen, the Prince and all the Royal Branches, with the Nobility, Clergy and Commons of England, then assembled in Parliament, by Popish treachery appointed as sheep to the slaughter, in a most barborous and savage manner, beyond the examples of former ages." After 1846 the service was used less and less. In 1859, Parliament abolished it.

Home from the Wars
Inexpressible joy greeted the news of victory at Waterloo in June 1815. Napoleon, "the enemy and destroyer of the world's peace" had been finally defeated, bringing to an end years of anxiety and hardship. All over the country there was great rejoicing and the people of Denton must have felt especially proud of Samuel Hardy who was wounded in the great battle. Born at Bight Bank (the steep part of Stockport Road where it is joined by Scott Road) in 1791, he was the second son of William Hardy, a carpenter and in early life was apprenticed to a noted local shoemaker named Thomas Shaw of Three Lane Ends.[2]

"On the expiration of his apprenticeship young Hardy joined the militia and in 1813 volunteered into the 52nd Light Infantry. The colonel of this famous regiment was Sir John Colborne, afterwards Lord Seaton, and under him Hardy took part in the fierce fighting, at Nive, Toulouse,

[1] Middleton: page 130.
[2] We are following Middleton's account (page 133). Although he was buried in Denton Chapelyard in 1865 the Baptism Register contains no mention of him.

Orthes and Nivelle. But it was at Waterloo that the 52nd covered itself with glory, for it fell to Colbourne to lead the advance which determined the fortunes of the day.

"When the columns of the Imperial Guard were gaining the summit of the British position and were forcing backwards one of the companies of the 95th, Colborne, noting the danger, started the 52nd on its advance. The Duke of Wellington, who witnessed the movement, instantly grasped its importance and sent orders to Colborne to continue it. The 52nd cheered and went into battle with a rush that the French columns could not resist. In this charge, which has been classed as one of the most brilliant in the annals of the British Army, Hardy was disabled by a musket shot in the arm.

"On his return to England he resumed his old trade as a boot and shoe-maker and gained some distinction as a military bootmaker. In 1820, whilst billeted at Derby he fell in love with a farmer's daughter and having purchased his discharge, married and settled down as a shoemaker in Haughton. In 1858 he was awarded a pension of 6d. a day, afterwards augmented to 9d. a day. He died on April 10th, 1865 and was buried in the graveyard of Denton Old Church."[1]

An Astonishing Library

As the years went by at Wilton House, Parr Greswell gradually built up an impressive library. Books were a passion and he spent all the money he could afford on them. He was particularly interested in old and rare volumes – first editions from the oldest printing houses of Europe. By the time he died he had hundreds and it took six days to auction them off at Sotheby's in 1855. The total receipts of the sale were £758.6.6. but when we look at the catalogue and see some of the works he owned, without doubt they would have fetched many thousands of pounds today.

It was first and foremost a *CLASSICAL* library, containing many editions of all the ancient Greek and Latin authors. Take, for example, item 219: ARISTOPHANIS COMEDIAE, GRAECE.[2] The catalogue then adds a note "RARE, fine copy in morocco extra, joints, gilt edges. Paris AEgidius Gormontius 1528. This copy sold for £7.7s. in Dr. Heath's sale." Here then, was a rare book, printed in Paris in 1528, and highly valued but at the auction of Parr Greswell's books it was bought by a Mr.

[1] This detailed account is a perfect example of Samuel Hadfield's work as a local historian. He would hear it from Hardy's lips and pass it on to Middleton.
[2] *The Comedies of Aristophanes* (c. 445–385 B.C.) in Greek.

Wallor for the appalling price of 4s. 6d.[1] Something went badly wrong at the sale. A great library disappeared for a fraction of its value.

"Scarce" and "rare" appear regularly throughout the sale catalogue as also do notes such as – "This edition was rigidly suppressed by the Doctors of the Sorbonne."[2] There are works in Italian, French, German, Hebrew and Persian besides those in Greek, Latin and English. Surrounded by parishioners who were frequently illiterate, the erudite Parr Greswell quietly persued his studies. Oliver Goldsmith's description of a village parson must have been more than appropriate:— "And still they gazed and still the wonder grew,
That one small head could carry all he knew."[3]

Parisian Typography

The direction which these studies took was quaint indeed. Whilst collecting old books, Parr Greswell developed an interest in the origins of printing, more especially that printing which began in Paris in the fifteenth century. It interested him so much that he wrote a book on the subject and had it published by Cadell and Davies of London in 1818. It was called ANNALS OF PARISIAN TYPOGRAPHY and told the story of how printing first began in Paris. For it he had twelve fine woodcuts made, showing the heraldic devices of leading French publishers and these proved expensive. Not surprisingly the "Parisian Typography" did not sell speedily and we find him writing to Thomas Cadell with some anxiety.

"Denton near Manchester
Nov. 1st 1824"

"My dear Sir,"

"I received your favour of the 28th ult. and have this day come to Manchester in order to forward to you a Bill value £42.14.6d. drawn on Messrs. Curries Rankes & Co. Banker London and payable at sight.[4] This Bill I have specially indorsed to you and you will receive it inclosed in this letter. I have not received the Bales but hope they will soon arrive and that I shall find the Copies have received no damage either by lying in your warehouse or by Carriage hither.

Will you allow me to enquire whether the Octavo Editions of Mr. Roscoe's Lorenzo and Leo X still on your hands are numerous and

---

[1] Catalogue of the sale of Parr Greswell's books by Messrs. S. Leigh, Sotheby & John Wilkinson at their house in The Strand, February, 1855, page 15.
[2] Catalogue, page 34.
[3] Oliver Goldsmith (1728–1774), *The Deserted Village*.
[4] What an enormous amount of money to spend on books. They are possibly rare and will arrive packed in the bales referred to later.

whether they are likely to experience in Sale a depreciation anything like that of my unfortunate Book. With regard to Copies of Parisian Typography now remaining with you I observe your letter of October 13th ult. states the numbers 9 Large Paper 36 small. If you advise the selling them all to One individual I would accept 7/- a copy for the small or 7/6 for the Large and small together. I am greatly out of Pocket by that publication which cost a considerable sum in getting up particularly on account of the numerous wood cuts for which and for working them off I paid liberally. In a word – if you think it best to dispose of the 45 copies now in your hands in the way you mention I am writing to leave the price to you and to accept what you advise. I wish to ask would it be possible to obtain from you in exchange for them a copy or two of the Octavo Lorenzo and Leo or any other works which might be useful to me. These enquiries you will perhaps be pleased to answer when you acknowledge the receipt of the inclosed Bill."

> "I remain dear Sir,
> Yours very respectfully,
> W. Parr Greswell."

"In haste from
Messrs. Clarke, Manchester."[1]

Two months later a reply arrived from Thomas Cadell. No one had yet been found to buy the remaining copies of Parisian Typography whilst Mr. Roscoe's books on Lorenzo and Leo X had sold so well since they were published in 1800 and 1806 that the printers were at work on a sixth edition of the former and a third edition of the latter![2]

The Honoured Friend

Parr Greswell could proudly claim to be a friend of the great William Roscoe (1753–1831). He was Liverpool's leading citizen and a courageous political reformer. Born and bred in that city he had worked his way up to become a successful attorney, financier, philanthropist, scholar and poet. In 1800 he had published a Life of Lorenzo de Medici[3] in three volumes which was so successful that it created something of a renaissance in Italian studies amongst English scholars. A large number of clergymen in remote parishes were inspired to produce works on Italian drama, poetry and

---

[1] This letter is in the British Museum archives.
[2] Cadell to Parr Greswell, December 27th, 1824, British Museum.
[3] Lorenzo the Magnificent, the Florentine Prince who was also head of a House of immensely powerful merchant bankers. Leo X was a notorious Pope.

history. Parr Greswell tried his hand at translating the poetry of Angelus Politianus and others. The results were poor and lifeless judged by modern standards, but he was attempting to render the original into the kind of smooth verse of which Dr. Samuel Johnson would have approved. So as early as 1801 his MEMOIRS OF ANGELUS POLITIANUS had been published in Manchester.

This book, which was enlarged for a second edition in 1805, was described at length in the *Monthly Review* for October 1801. It is dealt with very kindly and politely and commended as of interest to "all lovers of sound learning and classical taste", but at the end of his six page review the writer feels constrained to pen these words:— "We are sorry that critical integrity obliges us to qualify our praise by censure of any kind; but, in perusing these compositions, our ears have been frequently offended by dissonant rhymes, which deform verses that in all other respects are beautiful. A few may be specified for the author's consideration:

Embrace Release	Essays Please	Ear Prayer	Leads Blades	These are good rhymes only in Ireland.
Defile Soil	Smile Toil			These are provincial rhymes. In Cheshire and Lancashire smile is pronounced *SMOIL*
Lore How	Couch Approach			These are rhymes nowhere."[1]

In 1806 Roscoe published his LIFE AND PONTIFICATE OF LEO THE TENTH in six volumes. It was extremely successful and much admired, although producing a certain amount of controversy. Knowing of Parr Greswell's library, he wrote to him in June 1806, asking if he could borrow two books he wanted to consult. "I wish to have a sight of these books before I print off the preface to the 2nd Edition of Leo, in which I have refuted the opinions of my critics about the letter of Luther of the 6th April." (Parr Greswell obligingly sent them by the Manchester coach.) Roscoe adds, "When shall we have the pleasure of seeing you again at Allerton? We hope for it this vacation."[2]

[1] *Monthly Review:* October 1801, pages 139–145. Parr Greswell, who was born in Cheshire, would speak with a northern accent.
[2] Letter of W. Roscoe to W. Parr Greswell, 22nd June, 1806, in possession of Professor D. H. Weinglass, University of Missouri, Kansas City, U.S.A. I am indebted to Professor Weinglass for a great deal of information about Parr Greswell.

A Portrait of Pope

How often Greswell and Roscoe met it is impossible to say but we know that Parr Greswell felt himself honoured by the friendship and his admiration for Roscoe was undisguised. We are not surprised to find him writing to congratulate him when yet another book appears – an editon of the works of Alexander Pope (1688–1744).

"Denton near Manchester
Aug. 15. 1825"

"My dear Sir",

"Since I had the pleasure of seeing you I have perused with great attention and interest the first volume of your Edition of Pope's works and it appears to me that you have not only bestowed immense pains upon the Biography of that distinguished Poet but also done him ample justice. Imagining as I did before that few additions could be made to the particulars concerning him which had previously been collected it was not without considerable surprize that I found you had drawn from his correspondence and the few other sources open to you such a full and well digested account of his Life and literary History. With regard to the Poet's moral character I should think your vindication perfectly satisfactory to every candid reader. I have not indeed read Mr. Bowle's Life nor any part of the controversy which it has occasioned – but when I perused his aspersions as brought forward and examined by you I felt not a little surprized that any Gentleman and scholar could deal so illiberally as Mr. B. seems to have done and attempt to elicit charges so injurious from evidence and circumstances so slight and equivocal. If on such grounds it would be considered criminal to stigmatise the living certainly it is still more so to libel the dead. The friends therefore of Equity and Justice (wheresoever they are to be found) have reason to rejoice that the immortal Bard who gave harmony and sweetness to our numbers has at length met with an able vindicator. And now speaking of harmony let me ask you whether you think the story is true that Pope had no ear or relish for Music – for though I cannot tell where I have read or heard that asserted – the impression has long been upon my mind that I have read or heard it. Is it possible that so sweet a Poet could be insensible to the charms of vocal or instrumental music? This would be indeed a paradox. I think those who are born with ears so Baeotian never can be Poets.

42

"Before I conclude let me mention that I disposed of the Prospectuses of your elegant Botanical work as it was intended. One of them was sent to the Librarian at the College the other I included in a Letter to Lord Wilton the day before the last meeting of the College Trustees mentioning how proper and desirable I thought it that such a work should be added to the Botanical Class in the Manchester Library.

"I am glad to say the work was immediately ordered by the Trustees on Lord Wilton's mention. I understand the Libraian has put the Order into the Hands of Messrs. Robinson & Bent respectable Booksellers in Manchester and probably known to you.

"Believe me my dear Sir always
"Yours most respectfully and faithfully,
W. Parr Greswell."

The desire to visit "respectable booksellers" must have drawn Parr Greswell from his parish on numerous occasions and luckily, an account of one such visit to Manchester from his own hand has been preserved for us to read. Here he is writing to Roscoe six months after he had sent him his congratulations on his biography of Pope.

"Denton near Manchester 23rd Jan. 1826
"My dear Sir,
"The receipt of your kind and most acceptable Letter permits me no longer to defer the fulfilment of an intention which I have sometime since formed of writing to you. Concerning the Picture which to my great gratification proved an agreeable present to you – our esteemed friend Mr. Shepherd would probably anticipate what I have to say – viz that being formerly in the frequent habit of intercourse with Thomas Falconer Esqr. of Chester who in the days of my juvenility bore a high reputation as a literary character and an encourager of studious young Men I had frequently noticed particularly a Portrait of Pope in his possession. After my removal to Manchester I saw little of Mr. Falconer but know that at his decease his establishment was broken up and presume that by order of his Executors the Picture in question with many other articles must have been sold by auction. In one of my late rambles about the Streets of Manchester entering an old book shop – I observed the Picture now in your possession – and instantly and as it were instinctively said to the master of the shop Where did you get that Portrait of Pope ? The recogniton was that of

43

an old and familiar acquaintance, though nearly 40 years must have elapsed since our last meeting so natural and spontaneous as to forestal every kind of doubt or question whether it were or not the identical Picture which Mr. Falconer formerly possessed. I found it indeed battered and worse for time and ill usage as we are apt to become ourselves. The Man could give me no satisfactory account of its migration – the incidents of them must remain a secret – nor had he probably any previous knowledge of its being a portrait of Pope excepting that he told me another person had so denominated it, before I had seen it. I immediately secured it with the pleasing intention of sending it to you provided any judicious friend should pronounce it worth your acceptance — for as to myself I certainly am no connoisseur in such articles. Fortunately Mr. Shepherd came to Manchester – and gratified us with a short visit here. This was the very opportunity I desired and as you are pleased to confirm his judgement – I am delighted that this Portrait by so singular a chance has at last fallen into those hands where the Poet himself could he now form a wish on the subject would doubtless desire to have it placed. With regard to the letters in the Bodleian you may I believe rest assured that there are none that affect the question of Pope's character besides those which my Son Richard copied and sent to you and from them every candid judge must agree with you that it incurs no danger. My Son Richard Fellow and Tutor of Worcester College Oxford is particularly intimate with Dr. Bandinell keeper of the Bodleian and nothing would give him greater pleasure than to introduce you to the Doctor and the Library if you could visit Oxford or if not – to render you any little service there he could perform. I feel much interested by your mention of the new Editions of Lorenzo and Leo – and wish I could conveniently have visited Liverpool this Xmas not from the convictions that my humble suggestions could as you are kindly pleased to say – be of any use – but certainly because a short interview with you would – as it always has done – have given me great pleasure.

"I had the pleasure of hearing recently of the marriage of on ofe your daughters and intreat you to make her the old fashioned but on my part very sincere Compliment of Wishing her much happiness, and believe me dear Sir

"Yours respectfully and faithfully
W. P. Greswell."

44

The Rural Poet

By now Parr Greswell must have realised that he would never publish a work which could bring him the sort of acclaim which Roscoe had enjoyed, but nevertheless, he pressed on quietly and brought out a VIEW OF THE EARLY PARISIAN GREEK PRESS in 1833. It would be hard to think of a book with a more limited appeal! He was back on his old, familiar ground – the origins of printing in Paris – but this time he confines himself to *Greek* works printed therein! It was a work of abstruse scholarship which only a tiny circle of expert classicists could appreciate, but no doubt he derived a great deal of personal satisfaction from it.

If we cannot follow him into the mazes of the Parisian Greek Press, we can, nevertheless, savour the modest little volume of poems which he wrote in odd moments over many years and finally published in 1832. The first and most important poem was called "The Monastery of St. Werburgh."[1] It told, in forty long verses, the story of the great monastery which was finally dissolved by Henry VIII and became Chester Cathedral. The poem is full of historical allusions which could only be grasped by a reader with a very good knowledge of history but the interesting thing about it for us is the way in which it shows his dislike of Roman Catholicism and monasticism in particular. Here, for example, is a stanza in which he argues that the solitary life of a monk is the very opposite of what Christ expects from his followers:—

> "With meditative gaze, the Minstrel viewed
> Each passing scene; and questioned much his mind; –
> Fulfills Man Heaven's behests in solitude,
> More dear to God as more he shuns his kind?
> Not so the Saviour deem'd – In every place
> Where Man resorted, there his presence found
> It's happiest sphere; diffusing widely round
> Example's brightest light and Virtue's loveliest grace."[2]

He was obviously proud of "The Monastery of St. Werburgh", but it is really very heavy and dull. If that were all he wrote his poetry would not be worth mentioning, but in the 1832 edition are two poems which deserve to be quoted in full. The first of these is "The Village Hostess" and it shows us Parr Greswell making a creditable attempt at being a rural poet in the style of Thomas Gray. Gray was a pedantic Cambridge scholar who had one great claim to fame – he composed the "Elegy Written in a

[1] First printed by itself in 1823 by Henry Smith of St. Ann's Square, Manchester in a very limited edition for circulation amongst friends. Published again in 1832 with the other poems referred to below.
[2] Stanza XXXVII of The Monastery of St. Werburgh by The Revd. William Parr Greswell, 1832.

45

Country Church-yard" in 1751. If imitation is the sincerest form of flattery, we can be certain that Parr Greswell's admiration for Gray must have been unbounded, for "The Village Hostess" is so similar to the famous Elegy, both in style and content, that it cannot be read without continually reminding us of its parentage. Nevertheless, it is an interesting and fascinating poem, every line of which could well have been true of Denton.

THE VILLAGE HOSTESS

Scene – a Country Church-yard.

TRAVELLER – VILLAGER

———

TRAVELLER

Beneath this quivering Pine's uncertain shade
    Methinks unwonted verdure decks the mound,
And every simple wild flower has display'd
    Its loveliest hues, and sheds its fragrance round:
    And lo! a stone just peeping from the ground
Silver'd with moss its venerable head,
Denotes the neighbouring mansion of the dead.

Say, Villager! what mortal moulders here,
    Beneath the heaving turf's perpetual green?
Less envied far, in humid vault and drear
    Imprison'd sleep the sons of pride, I ween,
    Than thus, beneath the ethereal arch serene,
Where, whispering soft, the tall Pine seems to wave
In guardian semblance, o'er the hallowed grave.

VILLAGER

Stranger! by chance or holy purpose led
    Where consecrated bounds these guests inclose
Sleeping in still seclusion, gently tread,
    Nor violate thine ancient friend's repose:
    For still her name the rude, brief legend shows,
 Ere-while to many a weary traveller known;
Read then (for thou canst read) the sculptur'd stone.

TRAVELLER

Ah! well I mark the name to pilgrims dear
    As to the withering herbage genial rain;
Of gentlest manners, and of heart sincere,
    In happier times the friend of all was JANE,
    Her home the haunt of every village swain,
Not there, for riot met the rustic band;
Toil sought relief, and Friendship converse bland.

As near her board, with foaming honours crown'd,
    Engag'd in social chat or sage debate,
Passing their glass of sparkling liquor round,
    The politicians of the hamlet sate,
    How wisely they retriev'd the sinking state!
Held the long parley! wing'd the pointed jest!
While boisterous Mirth his loud applause express'd.

There paus'd the wandering Jew: the patient Scot
    Belated there unbound his cumbrous load
Far borne and painful: – each his toils forgot,
    As each her hospitable threshold trod:
    In sooth, it was meek Courtesy's abode:
Told but the woe-begone his tale of grief,
And ne'er did JANE withold the prompt relief.

VILLAGER

Aye– many a mortal of the vagrant train
    Wilder'd by night with weariness opprest,
When howl'd the wind, when beat the driving rain,
    Found unbought shelter there, refreshment, rest.
    She ever lov'd to succour the distrest,
Condemn'd by friendless penury to rove,
Or stern mishap, or ill-requited love.

And when poor Robin, herald of the year,
    Proclaim'd the glad approach of festal day,
Shrovetide, or Easter, Wake, or busy Fair,
    What Hostess has thou seen like her, display
    Each culinary vase in bright array?
What dainties vied with her's to allure the taste?
Who spoke so kind a welcome to the feast?

47

But chiefly ere the dawn when angels told
    To wondering shepherds a Redeemer born,
Lustrations pure and rites ordain'd of old,
    Conspir'd her simple mansion to adorn:
    Then rural neatness usher'd in the morn
With bays and holly, and immortal yew,
Of Heaven's unfading bliss the emblem true.

Fail'd not to assemble there our choral throng,
    With minstrelsy attun'd to holy rhyme,
Chaunting as festive joy inspir'd the song,
    Each psalm and carol sacred to the time:
    There maiden fair, and swains in youthful prime,
As love inspir'd, and music's thrilling sound,
Join'd the gay dance, with many a whirl and bound.

There too, in martial guise and rustic phrase,
    The stripling mimic tales of terror told,
Stalking in arms grotesque and vizard face,
    As erst Saint George and other champions bold:
    How hardy Jack the Giant's might controll'd,
How courteous knight reliev'd the Fair distrest;
Till kindred ardour fir'd each youthful breast.

Oft have I heard the pageant train rehearse
    Harsh sounding names, and deeds of glory done,
And tell in many a legendry verse
    Of dragons vanquish'd and of battles won.
    And lo! the dire encounter is begun,
See the proud victor spurn the prostrate slain,
And see the vanquish'd rise to fight again.

Oft near her cheerful hearth the wily dame
    Expert in secrets deep and Fortune's lore;
To listening maids would solve some mystic dream,
    Or in the tell-tale hand their loves explore;
    Such were our artless joys in days of yore,
Ere vanish'd at suspicion's dark control
Nature's prime grace, simplicity of soul.

TRAVELLER

Kind SWAIN! I mingle my regrets with thine,
    But haste forbids my feet to linger here:
Thee too thy rustic labour calls, – be mine
    Dropping o'er this lone grave the pitying tear,
    To urge on my way, now shelterless and drear:
We mortals are but pilgrims of a day,
Here we just stop and rest: then pass away:

Short is our stage; and transient is the date
    To man assign'd his wilder'd race to run:
But who can tell, in this eventful state
    What sorrows shall obscure his setting sun,
    And dim the hours in cloudless morn begun!
Life's faithless joys what gathering ills deform!
How oft on sunshine waits the inclement storm!

VILLAGER

FAREWELL! but hear: On her declining age,
    Misfortune frown'd, nor merit's self could save,
Misery's keen pang neglectful to assuage,
    Cold CHARITY prepar'd her scanty grave.
    Not such the dole, her warm compassions gave,
Ere freezing want the generous wish repress'd;
And check'd the sigh that labour'd in her breast.

But yet if virtue claim the willing song;
    If honest praise on rural worth await;
Aye, yet, – full oft the listening youths among,
    Shall many a hoary swain lament her fate
    And as this path he treads in pensive state,
Sigh o'er her name, and halcyon days of yore,
Till busy memory sleeps to wake no more.

———

What we look for in vain in Parr Greswell's poetry is political comment.
Gray's elegy contained it; The Village Hostess does not. The theme of
Gray's poem is the lot of the poor, destined to live their lives in obscurity

because they are denied educational opportunity and their personalities are stunted by penury. He looks at the graves of "the rude forefathers of the hamlet" and wonders what they would have been capable of if only they had been given the chance. Then he admits that in their small way they might have achieved something.

Perhaps . . . "Some village Hampden, that, with dauntless breast,
      The little tyrant of his fields withstood."

John Hampden, a seventeenth century squire of Buckinghamshire refused to pay twenty shillings Ship Money tax to Charles I when he had dismissed Parliament and was ruling the country without it. Hampden became a symbol of the small man standing out against despotism in the name of individual liberty. Parr Greswell seems to have had no such heroes in spite of the fact that he considered himself a friend of William Roscoe. This is strange for Roscoe wrote many political poems and was widely loved or hated for them. In particular his "Wrongs of Africa" drew attention to the horrors of slavery against which Roscoe was a life-long campaigner. He was even attacked in the streets of Liverpool by a gang of rough seamen who knew he was an abolitionist. For a short time he was a Member of Parliament and was able to vote in support of Wilberforce's bill to end slave trading in 1807.

It is sad that Parr Greswll did not throw in his weight with Roscoe. It would have meant, of course, that he would have had to face bitter opposition from members of his own congregation, especially his social superiors like George Hyde Clarke, but this is what a Christian Minister is ordained to do. Prophets who would condemn injustice were badly needed, but, alas, Parr Greswell was not one of them. He turned to his books and let the world go by.

A Village Wonder

About noon on Tuesday, February 1st, 1714–15, "there happened a violent and terrible storm of wind which shattered and blew down the highest and greatest part of the yew tree in the Chapell yard which before was supposed to be one of the noblest and largest in the kingdom, being a very great ornament as well as shelter to the Chappell."[1]

When Parr Greswell came to Denton in 1791 the main trunk of the great tree was still standing, but it was in a very decayed state. It had never recovered from being torn apart by the sudden gust of wind 76 years earlier. People said that its branches had extended in one direction over the chapel roof and in the other over the lych gate (which was, however,

[1] Register.

50

nearer the chapel than it is today. The graveyard has been enlarged since the school was demolished.[1])

In 1800 someone cut the old tree down without permission. This caused a certain amount of indignation and George Hyde Clarke planted another young yew on the spot, built a stone circle round it and enclosed it with iron railings. But it did not survive. Today, a weeping ash tree, which looks to be some 40 years old, grows there, whilst on the stone circle the puzzled visitor can read: "This tree was planted and enclosed by George Hyde Clarke, Esq., of Hyde, A.D. 1801."

What a perfect subject for Parr Greswell, the rural poet! It gives him another chance to meditate on "the rude forefathers of the hamlet" sleeping in their graves beneath its shade. As he does so his imagination takes wing and he thinks he hears the tree speaking to him in its old, hoarse voice. It tells him of days when faith and zeal were stronger and God's people were in a better state of spiritual health. Here is the poem in full.

> While silent ages glide away,
> And turrets tremble with decay,
> Let not the pensive Muse disdain
> The tribute of one humble strain
> To mourn in plaints of pity due
> The fate of yonder blasted yew.
>
> Long blotted from the rolls of time
> The day that mark'd thy early prime,
> No hoary sage remains to say,
> Who kindly rear'd thy tender spray;
> Who taught its slow maturing form
> From age to age to brave the storm.
>
> Beneath thy widely branching shade
> Perchance his weary limbs were laid;
> Content, without a stone, to share
> The umbrage of thy grateful care;
> His utmost wish for thee to shed
> Oblivion's dews around thy head.

[1] A pencil note inside the front cover of the Burial Register (1813–1842) reads: "The ancient Penthouse over the large Gate Way into Denton Chapel Yard fell suddenly on the Evening of Thursday August 23rd 1838 about 6 o'clock. Supposed to be coeval with the Chapell."

And long thy darkling foliage gave
A hallowed stillness to his grave;
For there, if legends rightly tell,
No vagrant reptile dared to dwell:
E'en sprites, by moonlight wont to stray,
Scar'd at thy presence, fled away.

As thus, in contemplative mood,
The venerable trunk I view'd,
Forth issuing from the sapless rind
A hoarse voice trembled on the wind.
Amaz'd I stood, and wing'd with fear,
These accents caught my wondering ear – – –

"Me, to the precincts of the place
That antique hallowed Pile to grace,
From native woods, in days of yore,
The fathers of the hamlet bore. – – –
Foster'd by Superstition's hand,
A late memorial now I stand.

"My spreading shade, extending wide,
The village wonder – and its pride – – –
I mark'd, as years revolved, the blow
That laid each hardiest grandsire low – – –
Now worn with all consuming age,
I yield to Time's relentless rage.

"Nor fondly blame, with strain severe,
The simple zeal that placed me here.
Nor dare thy fathers to despise,
And deem thy upstart sons more wise.
Let self conviction check thy pride,
To error both too bear allied.

"Of Zeal's unletter'd warmth possest,
Yet still Religion fir'd their breast;
Frequent the hallowed court to tread
Where Mercy hears Repentance plead,
Constant the grateful hymn to raise;
Our Zion echoed with their praise.

"Their sons superior knowledge boast;
Knowledge how vain! since Zeal is lost.
Now, gradual as my branches pine,
I see Devotion's flame decline.
And while, like me, Religion wanes,
Alas! her vestage scarce remains."

The Old Band

Each year, November 5th gave the people of England a chance to express their patriotism and hatred of Popery. In Denton, there was a special service in the chapel, followed by bonfires, fireworks, heavy drinking and music from the Town Band. The Denton and Haughton Band, formed in 1818 when England was at peace once more after the Napoleonic wars, appeared publicly for the first time at the fifth of November celebrations. The townspeople – and especially the hatter Joseph Howard and the publican Robert Thornley – had subscribed generously to the appeal for funds. The band was able to buy a set of instruments, music paper and four instruction books from Robert Bradbury of Manchester, at a total cost of £210.

Then a quarrel broke out. Should it be called 'Denton and Haughton Band' or 'Haughton and Denton Band'? The question was settled for a time by painting "Haughton and Denton Band" on the big drum. Dentonians, however, were not satisfied with this and the first time the drum was repaired had the name altered to "Denton and Haughton Band".

Middleton's account (which we are following here), was undoubtedly taken wholly from what Samuel Hadfield told him in one of their long fireside conversations. When John Beeley 'the pride of the village' died in 1839 at the early age of 29, Hadfield was only fourteen, but he knew how great a loss it was. The funeral on December 20th was attended by a large number of local musicians because Beeley had been not only a member of the band, playing trombone and bugle, but also village school-master and organist at the chapel. On the following Sunday vocal and instrumential performers from Hyde, Ashton, Mottram, Stockport, Gorton and other places joined the musicians of the Denton and Haughton Band to pay a last, grand tribute to the memory of the dead schoolmaster. Young Samuel Hadfield was present on this occasion and says: "Ascending the chapel orchestra,[1] they performed several select pieces of music, amongst

[1] We now call it the gallery.

53

which was the Seventh Chapter of Job, when old Tom Sale, the tenor, made one of his best efforts. A suitable sermon was preached to a crowded congregation by the venerable village pastor, the Rev. William Parr Greswell."[1]

The Old Band went on for many years but in 1859 a rival, "Baxendale's Band", made its appearance. We know that the St. Lawrence's Sunday School Scholars' Walk was led by the Old Band in 1869, but gradually it was eclipsed by the new one. On that occasion it cost the Sunday School £5.10.0.[2]

Baxendale's Band went from strength to strength and is still with us today under its proper name – Denton Original Band. Its greatest achievement came on July 21st, 1900, when it won the thousand-guinea cup at the Crystal Palace.[3]

Parochial Duties

Parr Greswell worked extremely hard. One wonders where he found the time to study Parisian typography and write poetry. As well as teaching in his little grammar school he also did all the parochial duties until 1821. Besides the Sunday services there were baptisms and burials but *not* marriages. Denton was a chapelry and from 1754 to 1854 marriages were only solemnized in parish churches. So to be married you went to Manchester Parish Church (now the Cathedral) or to St. Michael's Ashton or to St. Mary's, Stockport.

Nevertheless, from our registers we can see how much work Parr Greswell had to do. In 1813, for example, the year in which a new register begins, he took 95 baptisms and 101 burials. What appalls the modern reader is that 73 of the burials were children and young persons under twenty-one! This was not in the least unusual. In those days, as can be seen from gravestones in the churchyard, infant mortality was extremely high and infectious disease could not easily be checked. Vaccination had been practised in England since 1800 but if we turn the registers over to 1853, when Parr Greswell was on the point of retirement, we still find the same pattern. There were 96 baptisms and 110 burials, 60 of which were of those under twenty-one, but to this must be added the deaths of several young adults.[4] Only in the 1920s does medical science really win the battle to save the lives of children.

[1] Quoted by Middleton on page 145. Parr Greswell was 74.
[2] Sunday School Treasurer's Account Book.
[3] Middleton: page 146.
[4] The Revd. Walter Nicol, Curate, took nearly all these services in 1853.

Owd Cobba's Funeral

Most of his duties would be unrelieved by any unusual circumstances, but Middleton[1] tells us of a funeral that was very different to most. John Taylor was the eldest of four brothers who were all colliers. He was nicknamed "Owd Cobba" and was esteemed as a prize-fighter. About the close of the eighteenth century he fought a desperate battle with John Slone at the Grapes Inn, Gee Cross and won. It was one of those brutal, bare-fisted fights which were so much admired by working men in those days and when he died in 1819 at the age of 53 Denton Band led the procession to the chapel playing "See the Conquering Hero Comes." Parr Greswell was so indignant that he ordered the chapelyard gates to be closed and refused to allow the burial party into the graveyard until the band went away. They did so playing "Kiss Me Lady."

Like Father, Like Son

William and Anne Parr Greswell had nine children. Like their parishioners they knew the sadness of losing them and they must have always regretted that neither of their daughters lived to marry. Sarah died in June 1802 aged three years and four months. When a second daughter was born in April 1805 they called her Sarah Anne, but she died when she was sixteen in August 1822.

With their sons they were much more fortunate. Five of them were to become very successful in their respective callings, but even so their eldest, Thomas Heamer, died in March 1819, when he was nearly twenty-four. This must have been a blow to his parents for he had shown great ability and had been, for a short time, Master of the Blue Coat School in Manchester.

With William, their second son, the story takes a much happier turn. After being educated in his father's little school he was sent to Manchester School and then to Oxford, where he became a Fellow of Balliol College. He had also taken Holy Orders so in 1821 we find him helping his father with parochial duties. Parr Greswell must have been very thankful to share the baptisms and funerals with his twenty-five year old son. William goes on helping, mostly in the University vacations, until 1829. He was then inducted as Minister of St. Mary's, Disley and hoped to marry a Miss Isherwood of Marple Hall, but she died whilst they were engaged. James Ralston, (whose letter is printed in Appendix III) was one of his church-wardens and a great friend. In 1837 he left to become Rector of Kilve in Somerset, where he stayed until his death in 1877.

[1] T. Middleton: page 139.

Edward, the third son, was to prove a greater help to his father than William. He also goes to Manchester School, after receiving Parr Greswell's tuition and then to Corpus Christi, where he was elected a Fellow and eventually became a Bachelor of Divinity. From 1825 we find him helping his father with baptisms and funerals and he continued to do so right into the 1840s, but mostly in the University vacations as Oxford was his true home and he lived the life of a scholar there until his death in 1869. He lies buried in the cloisters of Corpus Christi.

All this help from the family was excellent but how much better it would be if it were put on to a regular footing. Would one of them become a full-time Curate? Not Richard the fourth son, (born 1800) who was also an Oxford scholar and Fellow of Worcester,[1] not Charles (born 1802) who had decided against Holy Orders and became a surgeon practising in the Strangeways locality, but Francis Hague (born 1803) who was happy to be ordained and become Assistant Curate in 1829. Accademically he was in the same class as his brothers, having become a Fellow of Brazenose College that year. He took his first baptism on August 16th and proudly signed himself "F. H. Greswell, Assistant Curate and Fellow of B.N.C. Oxon."

The Resurrectionists

Newspapers of those days were full of lurid accounts of the Burke and Hare scandal. In January 1829 Burke was publicly hanged before a huge crowd at Edinburgh as an example to would-be body-snatchers. But these were also days of desparate poverty for very many, so not surprisingly, Burke and Hare's example found imitators. "Resurrectionists," as they were called, were known to operate from Manchester and when we read Dr. James King's description of the town, we can easily imagine the sort of ruffians to whom the idea of selling corpses for cash would appeal.

"The cottages are old, dirty and of the smallest sort; the streets uneven, fallen into ruts and in parts without drains or pavement; masses of refuse, offal and sickening filth lie among standing pools, the atmosphere is poisoned by the effluvia from these and laden and darkened by the smoke of a dozen tall factory chimneys.

"A horde of ragged women and children swarm about here, as filthy as the swine that thrive upon the garbage heaps and in the puddles. The race that lives in these ruinous cottages, behind broken windows, mended with

[1] He deserves a book to himself and is the man after whom Greswell County Primary School on Percy Road, Denton is named.

oilskin, spring doors and rotten doorposts, or in dark, wet cellars, in measureless filth and stench, in this atmosphere, penned in as if with a purpose, this race must really have reached the lowest stage of humanity."[1]

Some dark night in early February 1830, the body of Anne Booth, which had been buried on January 20th by Mr. William Greswell, was dug up and stolen. The body-snatchers made their way towards Manchester, but something went wrong and they dumped their burden, hiding it in a pile of manure at Gorton. One of Mr. Green's workmen at Gorton House discovered the sack containing the body when he was spreading the manure over a field. The sack, with the body in it, was placed in the manure again and a watch kept until midnight, in the hope of surprising the thieves when they returned to collect it. But they did not come. Probably they had realised that it was in too advanced a state of decomposition to sell to any surgeon for dissection. Next day an inquest was held at a public house in Gorton and it was soon discovered to have come from Denton chapel-yard.[2] On February 21st Mr. Parr Greswell buried her again. It was very probably from a pauper's grave that the corpse had been taken for she seems to have been without relatives able to give definite information about her. When buried the first time William Greswell entered her in the register as Anne Booth of Denton, 75 years, but Parr Greswell, at her second burial, entered her as Anne Booth of Haughton, 84 years!

In the middle of this sad farce, Francis Hague Greswell died. His curacy had lasted less than six months. He seems to have become ill at the end of November, when his signature is no longer found in the registers and on January 27th 1830 he died at the age of twenty-six. Six days later his elder brother William conducted the funeral.

Edward continues to help his father, taking time off from Oxford in addition to the vacations right on into the 1840s, but there is yet another son able to lend a hand. Clement, the last of the nine children, was born in January, 1809; he becomes a Fellow and Tutor of Oriel College, Oxford as well as taking Holy Orders. In March, 1837, aged twenty-eight, he helps his father in the parish from March to April.

A Stream of Curates

For William Parr Greswell the hard days were now over – and it was essential that they should be, seeing that he was in his seventies! Edward, who helped far more than any other son, is often in the parish for short

---

[1] Dr. James Kay: "Report on the moral and physical condition of the working classes employed in the cotton manufacture in Manchester."
[2] *Manchester Mercury*, March 2nd, 1830. Compare Middleton, page 55.

spells, but in 1838 a succession of curates begins to arrive. William Townsend Hozier (January 1838–1840). B. J. Clarke (December 25th 1850–June 1842); and George Jackson (September 1842–September 1846) were the first three.

As far back as 1815, Parr Greswell had told his Bishop that Denton Chapel was far too small for the needs of the community. It was disgraceful that nothing had been done to remedy this situation whilst the population had actually trebled! We know that Richard Greswell felt strongly about it and we can possibly detect his influence behind the fact that the fourth curate, Thomas Newham Farthing, comes in September 1846 to undertake the "working-up" of the newly marked-out parish of Christ Church.

Mr. Farthing, who was twenty-six, had been born in Kingston-upon-Hull. After graduating at Cambridge in mathematics and divinity, he was ordained in 1843 as assistant curate of St. Mattias, Salford. In Denton he had to start from scratch, building a church school, a church and a parsonage. Financially, he was greatly helped by Parr Greswell and his sons – especially Richard – but pastorally the task was a tough one. His first service was held in a club-room attached to a public house and the congregation consisted of about half-a-dozen, principally women and children.[1] Nevertheless, his success was spectacular and he stayed as Rector until 1872, when he went to Mossley. There he built New St. George's, which was consecrated in 1882.

Middleton tells us that he was a man of great energy and noted as a preacher.[2] He was also a Tory and strongly against Gladstone's Act of Parliament to disestablish the Irish Church in 1868. He became the Honorary Secretary of the Northern Church Defence Association, attending meetings and debating with dissenting ministers; arguing that the Protestant Church of Ireland (the equivalent of the Church of England) should remain established throughout the whole of Ireland. This meant that in spite of the fact that three-quarters of the population were Roman Catholics, they had to pay towards the upkeep of a Church which they rejected. Here is what the famous Sidney Smith[3] had to say about such a state of affairs:

"The revenue of the Irish Roman Catholic Church is made up of half-pence, potatoes, rags, bones and fragments of old clothes, and those *Irish* old clothes. They worship often in hovels, or in the open air, from the *want* of any place of worship. Their religion is the

[1] T. N. Farthing: *Six Sermons* (1889). His son Charles wrote a biographical sketch as an introduction.
[2] Middleton, page 77.
[3] 1771–1845.

religion of three-fourths of the population! Not far off, in a well-windowed and well-roofed house, is a well-paid Protestant clergyman, preaching to stools and hassocks and crying in the wilderness; near him the clerk, near him the sexton, near him the sexton's wife – furious against the errors of Popery, and willing to lay down their lives for the great truths established at the Diet of Augsburg . . .

". . . though I have the sincerest admiration of the Protestant faith, I have no admiration of Protestant hassocks on which there are no knees, nor of seats on which there is no superincumbent Protestant pressure, nor of whole acres of tenantless Protestant pews, in which no human being of the 500 sects of Christians is ever seen. I have no passion for sacred emptiness, or pious vacuity . . .

"For advancing these opinions, I have no doubt I shall be . . . called atheist, deist, democrat, smuggler, poacher, highwayman, Uniterian, and Edinburgh Reviewer! Still, *I am in the right*, and what I say, requires excuse for being trite and obvious, not for being mischievous and paradoxical. . . .

"I have always compared the Protestant church of Ireland . . . to the insitution of butcher's shops in all the villages of our Indian empire. 'We *will* have a butcher's shop in every village, and you, Hindoos, shall pay for it. We know that many of you do not eat meat at all, and that the sight of beef steaks is particularly offensive to you; but still, a stray European may pass through your village, and want a steak or chop: the shop *shall* be established; and you shall pay for it.' This is English legislation for Ireland!! There is no abuse like it in all Europe, in all Asia, in all the discovered parts of Africa, and in all we have heard of Timbuctoo!"[1]

Mr. Farthing's objections to disestablishemnt arose from his view of the Kingdom of God. He looked for a future in which the whole world would be completely Christian and the Christian convictions of the population of each country would be reflected in its Government. State and Church would be *ONE* – perfectly expressing the will of God. In a sermon he said "Melchizedek was *KING* of Salem: he was also *PRIEST* of the most high God. This union of temporal and spiritual functions was as common as it was natural. He who ruled the people in their ordinary life, taking the lead in directing, also, their religious affairs. This intimate and wholesome union of Church and State we find embodied in the Theocracy of the

[1] Sidney Smith: Fragment on the Irish Roman Catholic Church (published in 1845). Although the Church Rate had been abolished in 1833 large numbers of Irish Catholics in country areas still had to pay tithe-rents to the Protestant Clergy.

Jews."[1] No doubt, dissenting ministers pointed out to him that complete union of Church and State need not necessarily inaugurate an age of bliss. It was the Theocracy of the Jews which had plotted and carried out the crucifixion of Jesus Christ! But Mr. Farthing would not be impressed by this argument. He saw the issue in black and white and became deeply involved in it on an emotional level. When news came through in 1869 that Gladstone's Liberal government had passed the disestablishment bill, Mr. Farthing was taken seriously ill and could not resume his duties for thirteen weeks.[2] His hair and beard began to turn grey and he never again seemed to be as vigorous as he had been before. As for Gladstone – poor Mr. Farthing must have been appalled! When Christ Church was dedicated on October 13th, 1853, Gladstone – a friend of Richard Greswell's – had been present. In those days he was a Conservative and in favour of the Irish Church remaining established! But now, in Mr. Farthing's view, he had become disloyal and untrustworthy. It is true that Gladstone had his faults, but one of the things which made him a very great man was the ability to keep an open mind on many issues. He came to see the disestablishment of the Irish Church as an act of social justice and he acted with passionate sincerity as a Christian and a Churchman. Mr. Farthing, like many others, could

Thomas Newham Farthing,
First Rector of Christ Church.

[1] T. N. Farthing: *Six Sermons* (1889), Sermon III, page 52.
[2] T. N. Farthing: *Six Sermons* (1889), page 11.

not see the wood for the trees. To him it was an act of sacrilege and a sell-out to the Church of Rome!

All this disappointment made him a more convinced Tory than ever. In February 1869 he attended a meeting of the Denton and Haughton Constitutional Association at the Coach and Horses Inn, Hyde Road. In reply to a toast of The Bishops and Clergy he spoke of his political beliefs. "Free Trade and Richard Cobden the great advocate of it, have failed," he said. "Conservatism in politics and protection in trade was the only sound policy."[1] When this appeared in the *Ashton Reporter*, the Reform Union convened a meeting at the King's Head, Crown Point, "to vindicate Free Trade and Richard Cobden from the recent attack of Mr. Farthing."[2] A lively correspondence then followed in the local papers.

George Aspinall (January 1847–April 1849); C. N. S. Hayton (June 1849–March 1851) and finally Walter Nicol, were Parr Greswell's last Curates. In his remaining years they did all the parish work for him, but he presided at the monthly Holy Communion until his resignation in 1853.

St. Lawrence Appears

In 1839 restoration work was carried out at the chapel and Parr Greswell put up his famous inscription in Latin which is now on the left-hand side of the sundial. Originally this inscription was over the south-east door – a door which no longer exists because it was removed in the enlargement of 1872–73, but fortunately we have a photograph of it which is reproduced on page 104. The inscription reads:—

"STRVXIT RICHARDUS HOLLAND DE DENTON, ARMIGER,
      ANNO EDVARDI IV SEPTIMO
RESTITVIT PATRONI ET DIVERSORUM LIBERALITAS,
ANNIS M.D.CCCXVI – M.D.CCCXXXIX"

The translation is:—
"Richard Holland of Denton Esquire, built (this chapel)
      in the seventh year of Edward IV
Restored by the Patron and several other generous people in 1816 and
      1839."

The seventh year of Edward IV was 1468 and Parr Greswell was certainly wrong in thinking the building so old. Booker says that Parr Greswell was

[1] *Ashton Reporter:* 13th February, 1869.
[2] *Ashton Reporter:* 20th March, 1869.

misled by false information in volume IX of Briton and Bayley's "Beauties of England and Wales" (page 288) and that the indisputable date of the chapel is 1531–2.

We have no detailed information about the 1839 restoration but we know that "the workmen took out of the walls large pieces of plaster, which was found to be so hard as to bear cutting and polishing like marble, and was used to manufacture ornaments from, when polished it is like red granite."[1]

I have taken the above quotation from The Strines Journal. This was a monthly magazine written by Joel Wainwright and John R. Gregory. These two young men felt so isolated in their little village near New Mills that they decided to write a magazine. And *write* is indeed the word for they wrote it out in long-and hand passed it round amongst their friends like an ancient manuscript! As there was only one copy of each month's edition, it is amazing that any have survived, but all of them have been preserved and can be read on microfilm in the Local History Library, St. Peter's Square' They also put drawings and photographs in their Journal, thereby making it one of the most valuable sources of information we possess.[2]

From the article on "The History of Denton Chapel" it is obvious that the writer, who signs himself J.P.[3] knew The Revd. Edward Greswell, who was, by now, living at home with his old father. During the course of the conversation J(ohn) P(ollit) was given this piece of information: "The patron Saint to whom the chapel is supposed to have been dedicated is St. James, it has however since been discovered by The Revd. E. Greswell that the patron Saint is St. Lawrence."[4]

Booker is certain that it was St. James and that the Greswells made another mistake in attributing it to St. Lawrence. The story has been handed down that pieces of stained glass were discovered in the vestry on the north-east side of the church which was being used at the time as a lumber room.[5] When put together they showed St. Lawrence burning to death on a grid-iron and as his feast day is August 10th, co-inciding with Denton Wakes, the Greswells guessed that he was the patron saint. Who discovered the glass and when? It's possible that Edward did so whilst the 1839 restoration was in progress.

[1] *The Strines Journal*, No. 14. Vol. II, October 1853. The English grammar is J(ohn) P(ollit)'s!
[2] They began publication in September, 1852 and continued for eight years.
[3] It is probable that J.P. was John Pollit (1804–1854). He was schoolmaster from 1837 until his death. Joel Wainwright would ask him to write the article for the Journal.
[4] *Strines Journal*, October 1853, page 265.
[5] Middleton, page 47.

The earliest known photograph of St. Lawrences',
taken by Joseph Sidebotham in May 1853.

Denton Wakes

Before the coming of the railways in the 1840's the great majority of people spent holidays at home. Denton Wakes, in the second week of August, began with rush-bearing. First, the chapel received its annual cleaning and the old rushes were taken out. Then a rush cart was decorated with garlands and piled up with bundles of neatly-dressed rushes called "bolts". This cart was then taken in procession to the chapel and the fresh rushes were spread beneath the seats on the Friday before the Wakes.[1] On Wakes Sunday, morris dancers attended the service and Mr. Greswell preached a suitable sermon. The rushes helped to keep people's feet warm in winter and were convenient to kneel on.

The rest of the week was given over to enjoyment by the whole population. It was a time for spending money. There was a Wakes Fair at which the house-wife could do a great deal of buying in for the year and everyone who could afford it had new clothes. And then there were the organised entertainments and amusements. Horse, pony and donkey rides; foot races for both men and women; bull-baiting and cock-fighting. There were prizes, of course; silver cups, saddles, bridles, whips, dog

[1] Middleton, page 129.

chains, smocks and hats. In 1823, on the first Saturday of the Wakes "a match for a stake of £10, two miles, was decided on the new turn-pike road[1] between Crown Point and Gorton Toll Bar between Mr. Rowbotham's *Lively Sally* and Mr. James Ashworth's *Cork Eye*, won by the former. On Monday another match between *Cork Eye* and Mr. Knowles' mare, one mile, for £5 was easily won by the horse on the same road."[2]

There would be bull-baiting and cock-fighting at most Wakes until Parliament put a stop to it. We know that a bull, provided by Mr. Dakin of Salford, was baited at the Bowling Green Inn[3] during the Wakes of 1831. It was also baited the same year at Hooley Hill Wakes, when it tossed fat James Marlor of Newton.[4] It was a vicious business. The bull, chained to a post, was generally tormented by men and boys who hit it, prodded it with sticks or dared each other to go as near its horns as they could. But the main "sport" was provided by dogs which tried to bite the bull without getting hurt. The bravest dog's owner received a prize. It was an exhibition of ignorance and callousness which Parliament outlawed in 1835. Cock-fighting, which was no better, was made illegal in 1849, but it was harder to stop than bull-baiting because secret meetings could be held in barns and lofts. Middleton tells us that as late as 1888 a crowd of over a hundred gathered in a hay loft at Denton Hall to see a fight. However, the police got to know of it and climbed into the loft just as the organisers were about to start with ten couple of cocks.[5]

Cricket was a big feature of the Wakes. Interest in the game grew steadily from about 1800 onwards and the famous club at the Angel Inn was formed in 1824. In those days cricket was as closely associated with gambling as horse-racing is today. Not only would spectators make bets on the outcome of a game, but the clubs themselves challenged each other for large stakes. In May, 1837, the club at the Angel began its season with a dinner at which it announced that the team would play any eleven near Stockport for any sum of money. The membership was exclusive. The players were mostly hat masters and they had to be men of means in order to pay the opposing team if they lost the match and the bet. In 1840 there were only 49 active and 18 honorary members,[6] but they had a large following amongst the general public. Some of the players wore tall

---

[1] This new road had been made in 1818.
[2] Middleton, page 14 quoting the *Stockport Advertiser* of August 15th, 1823.
[3] This inn was originally called "The Blue Bow" or "The Blue Ball" – Middleton, page 129.
[4] Middleton, page 129.
[5] Ibid: page 129.
[6] Ibid: page 141.

beaver hats, but leg guards and gloves were not used. The ball was hard and the bowling chiefly underhand, but it could be both fast and effective.[1]

Middleton tells us that "The Sheffield Clown Cricketers visited Denton annually for many years. They left the train at Godley Station and then, grotesquely dressed, mounted on the backs of donkeys – the "Arabian ponies" of the advertisement – rode in procession through the streets of Hyde and Denton to the great delight of crowds of onlookers."[2]

They were obviously very successful in 1875 and the account in the *Ashton Reporter* helps us to see them clearly with our mind's eye.

"The chief attraction of the Wakes was Messrs. Casey and Robson's Clown Cricketers. The members of the Denton Cricket Club had for some years got up athletic sports at the Wakes but this year they made a happy change by introducing these celebrated clown cricketers. They were engaged for two days – Monday and Tuesday; and their great fame brought a large number of spectators to the field on each day. On Monday the number of spectators was specially large. The members of the Denton Club had made every arrangement for the accommodation, comfort and convenience of the public. Mr. Stanley, of the Old Soldier, had two refreshment tents on the field, and the Denton Band was present, and played at intervals. The Clowns were the first to go to the wickets, which they kept for nearly the whole of the day. They are good batsmen, and, in addition to that, they are most amusing in their antics; and their powers of repartee and of making the most of any and every circumstance that comes under observation are very great. Their dresses, too, bear out their profession of clowns, being most grotesque, and altogether they afforded a rich treat. Their score will be found in another column, and in saying they were too many for the local team it is not to be implied that our local men are not good cricketers. The Clowns had everything in their favour. The ground was in capital order on Monday, but on Tuesday, when the local team went to the wickets, it was very heavy through the rain. On Monday and Tuesday evenings the Clowns gave an entertainment in the Co-operative Hall. That on Monday evening was very well attended, and was a very rich treat. The entertainment was brought to a conclusion by an amusing sketch, entitled "The Happy Pair," by Mr. and Mrs. Lloyd Clarence, which was characterised by those who saw it as excellent. A somewhat similar entertainment was

[1] Ibid: page 142.
[2] Ibid: page 143, Column 1.

given on Tuesday, and the Clown Cricketers may be assured that if they come again to Denton they will meet with a most hearty reception."[1]

Again, one of the best descrpitions of the Wakes as a whole is the *Ashton Reporter's* account of 1874. We can do no better than let it speak for itself, so here it is in full:

"The Denton Wakes of 1874 are past and gone, and notwithstanding the depression of trade and the collier's strike, the festival has been characterised with the usual amount of fun and rejoicing. The weather has, as a whole, been unpropitious, but still it did not damp the ardour of those who are determined to make the most of the festive season. The fun commenced as usual on Saturday, but the afternoon being showery, the number of visitors fell somewhat short of those of previous years. Still the streets presented a lively appearance. The principal attraction was to be found on the Market Ground, which was wholly taken up by the itinerant caterers to the public taste. Indeed, the ground was found to be too small and many stalls had to be erected in the streets. Towards evening there was a tremendous din. The rifles at the shooting booths kept up a continual of pop, popping. The hurdy-gurdies screamed forth their discordant notes; the weklin rang with the more discordant bawls of the show folks, who did not seem to have the least mercy upon their lungs; and the whole Market Ground was one Babel of confusion and uproar. Of course, there was the usual complement of dobby-horses and swing-boats, and they were well patronised. Case's marionettes were a source of considerable attraction. Attached to this exhibition was a very good band, whose strains formed an agreeable contrast to the gongs and cracked instruments that made such a hideous din all around. Those who had a taste for theatricals could have it gratified at a cheap rate. Ferguson's circus afforded a variety for those who were that way inclined, and those who had an itching after the monstrous had only to pay the "great rat" a visit, and they would no doubt be satisfied. William's theatre of arts afforded an opportunity of study to those who have a taste for the "fine arts", and those who wanted to present their sweethearts with a representation of their sweet selves had only to sit for a few seconds, and the thing was done. As already remarked, the streets were all in a commotion. The boys availed themselves of the opportunity to try and "raise the wind". One batch perambulated the

[1] *Ashton Reporter*, 14th August, 1875. It sounds as if 1875 was the year of their first visit to Denton.

66

town, dressed up as morris dancers. The music to which they performed their antics was supplied from the mouth of one of them, who discarded all sorts of instruments, barring a triangle, at which he hammered away most unsparingly. He was accompanied in concert by another youngster, who kept thumping away at an old cracked drum. Another batch, somewhat similarly attired, paraded in a similar manner. They had two or three rifles, and the sound issuing from them had a little more pretentions to music than the other batch could boast of.

"The members of the Denton Cricket Club played a match with eleven "Wanderers", and as is elsewhere recorded, they were well patronised. On this occasion the local team fully maintained their reputation, for they scored 96 to their opponents' 29.

"The publicans, though a little chary this year about employing talent, were not altogether without. Mr. Robert Kirkpatrick had Mr. Charles Montague, the champion concertina soloist, and the old favourite, Mr. G. Guernsey, the celebrated comic vocalist. Mr. Montague is a most accomplished player on the concertina and the manner in which he played was simply astounding. Mr. Thomas Sheriff accompanied on the piano and harmonium with his usual ability. But the chief attraction at the hostelry was Mr. Carl Reid, the ventriloquist. Tommy and Joey performed their parts admirably. Tommy is a wonderful little fellow, and in the hands of Mr. Reid gives forth a most racy discourse in the true Lancashire dialect. The vernacular is rich, and the manner in which the dialogue is kept up proved that Mr. Reid is one of the first ventriloquists of the day. The array of talent here brought together collected full "houses", and Mr. Kirkpatrick had his due share of patronage. At the Nottingham Castle Mr. Rawding provided several attractions. There were several first-class singers, both local and foreign. Among the locals Mr. James Wilson of Dukinfield, held a conspicuous place, while Messrs. D. Oldham and Craig, both of Hyde, ably accompanied on the piano. Mr. J. Broadbent of the Jolly Hatters, was also well provided. Among the talent here engaged was Miss Carrie Griffiths, Miss Jenny Blanche, and Mr. Fred Marson, Mr. Henry Winterbottom acting as pianist. The other public-houses had their special attractions, and upon the whole there was plenty of variety to suit the most fastidious taste. Mr. George Kirkpatrick, of the Bowling Green, had the misfortune of having one of his children dead at the earlier part of the wakes, and this obliged him to give back orders to the artistes he had engaged.

He was, however, busy on the bowling green, and on Monday and Tuesday he had a portion of the Denton Original Brass Band playing in the house.

"Monday, as usual, was the busiest day, and on that day there was a large influx of visitors, and the streets were quite alive. The athletic sports, which were held on the cricket ground, were one of the principal centres of attraction, but the showery character of the day militated against them to a certain extent, and on Tuesday they had to be postponed in consequence of the rain. The colliers turned out on Monday with a cart loaded with coal and drawn by two grey horses. There was a number of men dressed in "Morris" garb, and they were accompanied both on Monday and Tuesday by the Stalybridge Amateur Band. They cast a fine dash and were followed in their perambulations by a large crowd, but it is to be feared that they did not find the public as generous as they could have wished. Towards evening the Market-ground presented a most lively spectacle. What with the popping of the rifles, the bawling and shouting of the show folks, and the pushing and "thrutching" of the crowd, the scene was very animating. It was to be feared that, on account of the hatting trade, the wakes would be a comparative failure, but to a person visiting the Market-ground on Monday, no signs of a scarcity of cash would appear. The pennies seemed to be rife enough, and the owners of the shooting galleries and hobby-horses did a roaring trade. One pleasing feature was observable, and that was the absence of drunkenness. While all did appeared to enjoy themselves, none seemed to indulge too freely.

"In Haughton Green too, the wakes kept up with great spirit. The innkeepers there had their special talent, and everything went as merry as a "marriage bell." As a whole, it may be said, that the Wakes of 1874 were a success, despite bad weather and the dullness of trade."

A Challenge from "Ranters"

In March 1840 two cottages were rented by the Primitive Methodists of Haughton Green and converted into a preaching room, also to be used as a day and Sunday School.[1] When news of this reached the Greswell family, it must have caused a considerable amount of annoyance. Primitive Methodists were "Ranters" – that is, highly emotional, tub-thumping enthusiasts, whose services were conducted by uneducated working-men

[1] Middleton: page 83, Column 1.

with Socialist inclinations.[1] Nor for them the worship of God, Queen and Empire. They preached Christ Jesus, the Friend of sinners and the champion of the poor – which is exactly what he is in the Gospels.

Primitive Methodism was born in 1810 at a huge open-air rally held on Mow Cop in Cheshire. It was a splinter movement breaking away from mainstream Methodism for social reasons. Primitive Methodists usually belonged to the lower or lowest orders of society and they felt emotionally alienated from Wesleyans, who had already become far too respectable, renting their pews, just as Church of England people did. "Prims" were making a genuine effort to reach out to the unchurched masses. Large numbers of the labouring poor "preferred standing at the street corners or assembling at the 'Point' to attending either church or chapel. There, throughout the whole of the Sabbath, men might have been seen, unwashed, in their working clothes, with their aprons rolled up and wrapped about their waists, either concocting a pigeon-fly or planning when and where the next flight was to be held, caring little for the means of grace; and if they noticed the places of worship at all, it was to insult those few who did attend, on their way to and from. To such an extent was this practised that it required no small courage for anyone to go to church or chapel whose home was so situated that the road lay through the toll bar or past the Crown Point."[2]

The words just quoted were spoken many years later by a Mr. S. Taylor at Hope Chapel Jubilee in 1886. They seem to contain genuine memories of the late thirties and early forties and help to show that there was a field in which the "Ranters" could profitably work.

It began to thrive at Haughton Green and such a challenge would not go unmet, so urged on by the Revd. B. J. Clarke, (Parr Greswell's second curate), some lay-people started a Sunday School in a cottage. It prospered so much that larger premises were needed and found in the club room of the Bay Horse Inn. It was officially opened by Thomas Rhodes on June 19th, 1842, which was the Revd. B. J. Clarke's last Sunday in the parish. Mr. Rhodes was Superintendent for three years.

Writing in 1855 Samuel Hadfield said:

"There are 135 scholars of both sexes who are conducted by their teachers to Denton Chapel the first Sunday in the month to morning service, which is considered by them a rich treat. The Revd. Walter Nicol of St. Lawrence's had procured the Bishop's licence and has

[1] "When Victorians talked of Ranters they meant Primitive Methodists" (Owen Chadwick, The Victorian Church, Vol. I, page 387).
[2] Middleton: page 83, Column 1.

commenced Sunday evening lectures in the temporary school-room which adjoins the Bay Horse Public House, a very unfit place for a schoolroom."[1]

The Select Vestries

"Moved by Mr. John Irwin, seconded by Mr. W. Wilcock that George Wilde, an idiot belonging to the Township of Denton be allowed the weekly sum of Two shillings to commence from this Date."
Carried

H. Briscoe
Chairman"

This was part of the business transacted in the School Room on Monday, November 11th, 1839.

Selected Vestries[2] came into being as the result of an Act of Parliament passed in the fifty-ninth year of the reign of George III (1819). They consisted of a number of gentlemen who were laypayers and householders, who met together (sometimes in the Chapel vestry, sometimes in the old School) to administer the Poor Law. Each year, at Easter, an *Annual Vestry* was held, at which a new set of gentlemen were re-elected by all the rate-payers of the Township. Needless to say there was very little change from year to year, but it is interesting to note that 1839 and 1840 were the last two years in which Parr Greswell served as a vestryman.[3] He was seventy and no doubt felt it was time to leave the work to younger men.

At the annual Vestry meeting two Overseers of the Poor were appointed, together with a full-time assistant Overseer, who was paid £36 per year and did the real work for the Overseers. There was also a Guardian of the Poor and two Surveyors of the Highways. The Select Vestry decided what the town's poor rate should be and collected it. It also rated all new property being built and administered poor relief to those who applied for it. Finally, they appointed one of the town's surgeons to visit "all sick paupers belonging to the Township within a circle of three miles from the Toll Gate, Denton, at a salary of seven pounds."

In February 1840 Denton Select Vestry laid a Poor Rate of 1/4d. on all rateable property but this proved insufficient and so another rate of one shilling was ordered in October. Still more money was needed in 1841 –

[1] Middleton: page 77, column 2.
[2] Denton and Haughton were two separate townships. They, therefore, had *two* select Vestries, both of which met in Denton Chapel Vestry or school or in the cottage nearest the chapel, which was a public house called "The Millstones". Sometimes both Select Vestries met on the same day. Unfortunately, all select Vestry Minute Books except one are now lost. Thomas Middleton, however, read several of them.
[3] As far as we know, later minute books are now lost.

rates of 1/4d. and 1/6d. being fixed in May and October. In 1842 it was 1/6d. in both May and October and in March 1843 it rose to two shillings in the pound.

This shows that the number of applications for Poor Relief was increasing but even so, Denton was certainly not yet burdened down with destitute people as some towns in the south of England were at this time. Nevertheless, life could be very hard as this entry of August 1851 shows:—

> "Ordered that Matthew Fieldsend, Widower with 6 children – wages 16/– per week – be allowed for the present 5/6d. and in four weeks from this date to have five shillings."

The Select Vestry also had the power to make this kind of order:—

> "Moved, seconded and carried that the Overseers be authorised to proceed against George Alcock and Thomas Cheetham in order to compel them to pay something towards the support of their illegitimate children."

That was in April 1840 but the fathers were obstinate. Thomas Cheetham has to be taken to court and in August 1840 we read:—

> "Ordered that Thomas Cheetham, Blacksmith, do pay the sum of 3/7d. per week towards the support of his Illegitimate Children and likewise all law expenses incurred."

Presumably he began to pay but George Alcock was more stubborn. Here is an indignant note from 3rd May, 1842:—

> "The Select Vestry do order and direct that George Alcock be promptly looked after and made to pay towards the support of Sarah Haughton's Child of which he is the father."

A Dispute with Doctor Massey

In 1842 the Poor Rate had risen to 1/6d. in the pound and the Vestry became acutely conscious of the drain on its resources. They drew up a list of persons to be summoned for arrears of poor rates, but their anxiety turned to indignation when Dr. James Massey, the surgeon appointed to visit all paupers, presented his bills. A special meeting held at 6 p.m. in the School Room on April 14th disallowed the following:—

Attending Gee's Family	..		..	5. 7. 0.
Ditto	Smith. H. Hill[1]		..	2. 16. 0.
Ditto	Artingstall's	..	..	1. 14. 0.
Ditto	Sellars		..	4. 19. 6.
				£14. 16. 6.

[1] Hooley Hill, now part of Audenshaw.

Dr. Massey instituted law proceedings against the Vestry so they paid him his money rather than go to court, but dismissed him from his position, telling him that from June 2nd "we shall not be responsible for any charge whatsoever for medical attendance upon any Pauper or Paupers who belong to the said Township." They also served a second notice upon him which shows just how reactionary and short-sighted the Vestry could be at times.

"We the undersigned Overseers of the Poor of the Township of Denton do hereby give you Notice that from and after the 2nd day of September next ensuing we will not allow any Charge for Vaccinating any person or persons in the said Township

As witness our hands

this 2nd day of June 1842

Isaiah Wilde

John Dearden Jr.   Overseers of the

Robert Cooke Jun.   Poor

Thomas Moss

Witness Zachariah Peacock"

But this foolish victory was short lived. Tempers cooled and at the next Annual Vestry on Monday 3rd April, 1843, Dr. Massey was re-appointed "Surgeon to the Township." At other times the Vestrymen could be in a much more generous frame of mind, as they were on February 7th, 1843, when they resolved "that Henry Renshaw's arrears of Poor Rates amounting to 15/- be forgiven him in consideration of the said arrears having been incurred at the time he and his family were bad of a fever." Some, however, felt there was little future for them in the England of the Industrial Revolution and the Select Vestry agreed:—

"Jane Bridgehouse' family to have 2/- per week till she goes to America."[1]

The Constabulary Force

There was no effective system of police in England until that provided by Sir Robert Peel for London in 1830. Further legislation in 1839 enabled County Constabulary Forces to be set up all over the country, financed through the rates. Some of the leading magistrates in Lancashire were men of progressive outlook and they took the opportunity to establish a County Force at once. Other parts of the country were often much slower and the West Riding of Yorkshire did not introduce police until 1856.

At meetings in Preston in November and December 1839, the magistrates decided to appoint 500 constables for policing the county under

[1] 28th June, 1842.

Chief Constable John Woodford. He was paid £500 per year, two assistant chief constables £200 each and thirteen superintendents £100 a year. Four hundred and eighty-two constables received eighteen shillings a week. The force was organised into fifteen divisions corresponding to the petty sessional divisions of the time.[1]

Middleton tells us[2] that the ratepayers of Denton agreed to accept the new "Rural Police Force", (as they called it), at a stormy meeting held in the chapel at which the chairman was Captain Clarke, R.N., J.P. of Hyde Hall. This must have been in 1839 and being a Justice of the Peace Captain Clarke would try to persuade the assembled company that their best interests would be served by agreeing to the new Force.[3]

He must have succeeded, for the Constabulary arrived, but within a year the Select Vestry decided to call a special meeting of all leypayers to give them an opportunity of "expressing their respective sentiments and opinions as far as respects having the present Police Force retained in the Township."[4] The meeting took place in the Vestry Room[5] of Denton Chapel on Monday, June 29th, 1840 at 4 p.m. with Dr. James Massey in the chair and decided to petition the Magistrates of the County to remove the Police entirely.

"To the Worshipful the Magistrates of the County of Lancaster in Quarter Sessions assembled.

"The Petition of the undersigned Rate Payers of the Township of Denton in the said County Sheweth That your Petitioners are convinced that the Rural Police force now stationed in the said Township is quite unnecessary and uncalled for.

"That the peace of the Township of Denton foresaid was as well or better kept with only one Constable before the Introduction of the County Constabulary force into the neighbourhood as it has since been.

"That even if the new system operating to its present extent were at all desirable the very great increase of taxation attendant upon it would in the present depressed state of trade fully warrant your Petitioners in the present requisition.

"Your petitioners therefore humbly and respectfully pray that you will be pleased in virtue of the powers conferred upon you by the

---

[1] *History of Lancashire Constabulary* (in duplicated form), page 1.
[2] T. Middleton: page 14, column 1.
[3] Middleton must have known and read a Denton Select Vestry Minute Book which ended in 1838. The only book the present writer has been able to consult is a Denton Select Vestry Minute Book beginning March 25th, 1839 and ending September 5th, 1843.
[4] Select Vestry Minute Book, 1839–1843.
[5] It must have been very crowded. The vestry was so small. Did they adjourn to "The Millstones?"

Act of Parliament in that behalf and with such consent as therein mentioned, altogether to withdraw the present Constabulary force from the said Township.

And your petitioners will ever pray."

This documnet lay in the School Room for a week for leypayers to sign and then was taken to the Quarter Sessions. But it failed and in March, 1841, another petition (this time called a Memorial) is sent to the Justices on behalf of *both* Townships – Denton and Haughton.[1] The Constabulary in Haughton met with the same opposition.

The wording of the Memorial is almost exactly that of the petition, making the point that two constables – one for Denton and one for Haughton[2] – had kept the Queen's peace adequately. These were the old village constables – men like Dogberry whom Shakespeare immortalised in *Much Ado About Nothing*. In theory any rate-payer could be compelled to be village constable for a year under the old law, but the job was usually done by some willing fellow who agreed to carry out the duties for a small salary on behalf of that rate-payer whose turn it was to hold the office. But the most basic point of all was "the very great increase in taxation . . . in the present depressed state of trade." The forties were to prove a bad decade for the whole country and especially for Denton. Reports of mass meetings, unrest and political protest were coming in all the time and the more enlightened justices knew that the County Constabulary would be needed.

The Price of Bread

Manchester, which had received its Royal Charter in 1838, was a centre of ferment against the Corn Laws. The working-classes were not interested in a Royal Charter; they wanted a '*People's* Charter'. On September 24th, an Anti-Corn law League was formed at the York Hotel and it quickly gained an immense following. Corn Laws had been introduced in 1815 to protect the British farmer against cheap imported wheat. The price of bread was kept so high that real distress and suffering was caused to the majority of the populaton. Farmers were content to see this state of affairs continue, but manufacturers were not. They openly sympathised with their work people. Cheaper food would help wages to go further and offset demands for rises.

Manchester was in a sorry state. In 1841, £2,800 was subscribed to a fund to celebrate the birth of Prince Edward, but when the organisers saw the hungry faces of the townspeople they decided that the money could not

[1] Probably the two Select Vestries of Denton and Haughton held a joint meeting on this occasion.
[2] Middleton gives their names: Constable Grimshaw for Denton and Constable Bowcock for Haughton.

be spent on festivities. Instead they used it to buy blankets and clothes for the needy.[1]

Things got worse. In 1842 there was rioting, not only in Manchester, but as near to Denton as Hyde and a new industrial weapon made its appearance – the strike. We are not surprised, then, to find Denton's Overseers of the Poor calling a special meeting of the Select Vestry in August "for the purpose of taking into consideration the present excited and unsettled state of the county and . . . selecting a number of the respectable residents to be sworn in as special Constables for the preservation of peace and good order."[2] They unanimously decided to appoint fifteen men and send a list of them to the magistrates. On September 22nd we find *both* select vestries meeting (in response to an urgent request from the magistrates of the division) to appoint 30 special constables – 15 for Denton[3] and 15 for Haughton.[4] Why? Had the Vestries not yet sent in their lists from their August meetings? Whatever the reason, the magistrates' demand is duly obeyed and we know that at a meeting on February 15th, 1843 Denton re-appoint their fifteen and five others volunteered to help them in any emergency which might arise.

Reports of unrest throughout the country continued and so in November, Denton Select Vestry, unanimously decided "to provide premises for a Lockups for the Township of Denton and also to appoint a fit and suitable person to have the charge of the said Lockups." They chose a house in Town Lane near the chapel, which became known as "The Court House" and had a convenient cellar at the back. Anti-corn law hooligans could now be put under lock and key and respectable rate-payers could sleep safely in their beds!

Sir Robert Peel was by now Prime Minister and although he had supported the Corn Laws, he now decided, to the consternation of his party, the Tories, that they must be repealed. This was a humane and socially just thing to do, but his fellow-Tories were furious. They turned against him and forced his resignation. Yet Free Trade was the right policy for Britain and greatly helped the country's economy to expand.[5]

Did the 'Memorial' of March 1841 sent from both Select Vestries succeed in getting the new Police force removed? Very nearly! On September

[1] John Sanders: *Manchester* (Rupert Hart-Davies 1967), page 119.
[2] Select Vestry minute book. The Revd. Thomas Horatio Smith was in the chair. He was the first Minister (1837–1843) of Hope Congregational Church which had been built in 1836.
[3] Select Vestry Minute Book.
[4] Middleton: page 29, column 2. Fortunately he has preserved the list of Special Constables from the now lost Haughton Select Vestry minute book.
[5] John Sanders: *Manchester* (Rupert Hart-Davies 1967), page 121.

Old Court House and Yard.

The Old Court House, showing jail

9th, 101 magistrates met in the Court House at Preston and voted that "the Police force should be abolished on the grounds of uselessness and expense." It was resolved, however, to delay a final decision for six months. Another meeting was then held at which 136 magistrates were present and they voted 81 to 55 that the force should be disbanded. But the County Police Act laid down that a Force could only be disbanded if the magistrates voted to do so by a 75 per cent majority! So the Government at Westminster won the day![1] Nevertheless, the rate-payers of Denton and Haughton were determined to hold on to their parish constables, so for a short time they were kept in being alongside the new force.

This seems to be the only explanation of a fascinating minute quoted by Middleton from a lost Haughton Select Vestry book. At a meeting on December 20th, 1843 "it was moved by Mr. Whitehead and seconded by Mr. Denerley that each constable be provided with a staff at the township's expense and to be considered its property. Also that two pairs of hand-cuffs be provided for the use of the said constables, at the township's expense, to be its property the same as the staffs."[2] Here was an attempt to make Constables Grimshaw and Bowcock look as efficient as the new Rural Police! But times were changing and try as they may they could not long put off the day when the Constabulary Force would be seen to be essential.

Silk Top Hats

The 1840's were known as the "hungry forties" and for good reason. The Corn Laws were not repealed until 1846 and Denton's hatting industry suffered its most serious depression during that decade.

Denton made *felt* hats. The silk top hat was known, but treated with contempt. In 1840 felt-hatting was very prosperous and production reached an all-time peak of 2,000 dozens per week. The population of the two townships had also increased to 6,759 – an increase of 4,258 in 40 years!

In January 1841, some Oldham hat-finishers went on strike because their firm was making abatements.[3] It was, however, at the same time paying the highest rates in the trade. The dispute spread rapidly all over South Lancashire and the Denton hatters, feeling that they deserved a greater share in the current prosperity, also came out. It was an appalling tactical blunder for they had failed to see that slowly fashion was already beginning to change. Hat-masters were determined to resist their employees and

[1] *History of the Lancashire Constabulary*, page 2.
[2] Middleton: page 30, column 2.
[3] The word is Samuel Hadfields's, *The Ashton Reporter*, September 13th, 1890, "Scrutator" No. 3. Does it mean redundancies?

some of them began to make silk hats. The upshot was that the strike collapsed, but not until it had dragged on for nearly four bitter months. The strikers had to return to work in the middle of May without a rise, only to find that the bottom had dropped out of felt-hatting. The silk hat was coming into fashion so rapidly that a recovery in trade was impossible. The number of hatting firms slumped disastrously. There had been twenty in 1825; there were only twelve in 1855.[1] Here is what Booker, writing in 1855, has to say:—

> "In 1847-8-9 the state of the Denton hatters and their families was pitiable in the extreme; their trade was now irrecoverably lost; upwards of one thousand families in Denton and Haughton were deprived for the most part of their subsistence and consequently, large numbers left the district in search of employment in other localities. Silk hats have now entirely superseded stiff ones and at the present time the manufacture of felt-bodies is nearly abandoned. The old established firm of Messrs. John Peacock and Bros. at present make not more than three dozen felt hats per week and these are principally of the class known as "rustics" and intended for exportation."[2]

If only we had a Select Vestry Minute Book for the late forties, how much it would tell us! But the only surviving one ends at September 1843.

New Schools, New Church

Richard Greswell, fellow and tutor of Worcester College, Oxford, took a keen interest in education and became Secretary of the National Society. This body had been formed in 1811 in order to provide schools for Church of England children. Its avowed aim was "that the National Religion should be made the foundation of National Education and should be made the chief thing taught to the poor, according to the excellent Liturgy and Catechism provided by our Church." Richard, a shy, nervous man, threw himself into the work of raising enormous sums of money with a will. First he gave a thousand pounds himself and then he wrote to all the noblest and wealthiest in the land from Queen Victoria downwards and succeeded in obtaining a total of £250,000. This was a tremendous achievement, enabling The National Society to lay the foundations of education throughout the country and, of course, Denton benefited.

Christ Church school cost £1,750. Work began in 1846, when The Revd. N. J. Farthing was made Curate with special responsibility for this

---

[1] D. M. Smith: *The Hatting Industry in Denton* (Industrial Archaeology, Vol. 3. No. 1, 1966).
[2] Booker: *History of the Ancient Chapel of Denton* (Cheetham Society 1855), page 13.

part of the parish. The school was opened on January 2nd, 1848 and Middleton shows us how most of the money was raised:—

Revd. Richard Greswell	.. ..	£250
The Revd. W. Parr Greswell	.. ..	£ 50
The Revd. Edward Greswell	.. ..	£ 50
The Marquis of Westminster	.. ..	£100
James Smith, Esq. ..	.. ..	£100
Council of Education ..	.. ..	£500
The National Society	.. ..	£350

The site was given by the Earl of Wilton[1] and Mr. Farthing took services in the school until the church was built five years later.

St. Lawrence's School, Stockport Road, was built by the Contractor, Mr. Bramhall of Manchester as soon as he had finished Christ Church. The school cost £1,660 and Richard Greswell gave nearly £1,000 towards it.

Christ Church was built from plans by George Gilbert Scott and cost £5,300. Once again the Greswell family was extremely generous.

The Revd. Richard Greswell	.. ..	£500
The Revd. W. Parr Greswell	.. ..	£100
The Revd. Edward Greswell	.. ..	£100
The Revd. William Greswell	.. ..	£ 50
The Revd. Clement Greswell	.. ..	£ 50
The Marchioness of Westminster ..	..	£100
Chester Diocesan Building Society..	..	£400
Incorporated Society.. ..	..	£400
Ecclesiastical Commissioners	.. ..	£250
Dean and Chapter of Manchester ..	..	£ 50
Edward Lloyd, Esq.	.. ..	£ 50
William Slater, Esq.	.. ..	£ 50
E. L. Sidebotham, Esq. ..	.. ..	£ 50
John Sidebotham, Esq. ..	.. ..	£ 50
Miss Woodiwis	.. ..	£ 50
William Peacock, Esq. ..	.. ..	£ 50
J. C. Harter	.. ..	£ 50

"The Earl of Wilton presented the site together with £100 and certain cottages worth £250 which stood within the limits of the proposed church-yard and which have since been demolished."[2]

One might ask, how could Richard Greswell afford to be so generous and the answer, in a word, is marriage. His wife Joana Julia Armitriding of

[1] T. Middleton: page 75, columns 1 and 2.
[2] Middleton: page 75, column 2.

Marston near Oxford, brought him a considerable fortune and projected him into high society. He gladly accepted his role as a Victorian Philanthropist and could be extremely shrewd at times. When, for example, he built Christ Church, he put up the tower first "and left it standing alone about four years, a wonder to all who saw it, quietly waiting . . . believing that wealthy churchmen would never let it remain long in this isolated state, and the event proved he was quite right.[1]"

All this activity came to a head on a very great day – Thursday, October 13th, 1853. In the morning Christ Church was consecrated by Dr. James Prince Lee, Bishop of Manchester, the sermon being preached by Dr. Samuel Wilberforce, Bishop of Oxford, who was son of the famous William Wilberforce. There was a crowded congregation and the collection was £427.

A cold collation was then served in the school across the road. The Earl of Wilton presided and there were speeches by the Bishops of Manchester and Oxford, The Revd. Richard Greswell and Mr. William E. Gladstone[2] who was then Chancellor of the Exchequer and a personal friend of Richard.

In the afternoon this distinguished company called at the old chapel and then proceeded down Stockport Road to the site of St. Lawrence's school. A large crowd had gathered to watch Miss Charlotte Anne Fletcher Fletcher[3] lay the foundation stone. She was seven years old and the only child of Mr. Jacob Fletcher Fletcher who had given the site. The Bishop of Oxford spoke briefly and led the people in prayer. Gladstone then mounted the foundation stone and made the following speech:—

"My friends, although I am reluctant to speak words among you which I am afraid must distract from the solemnity of those to which we have just been listening and in which I believe we have sincerely joined, yet it is a matter of no small pleasure to me to assure you that I rejoice to meet this great assemblage of the inhabitants of this vicinity,

[1] Wainwright Manuscript.
[2] Gladstone, who was nearly 44 when he visited Denton, began his political career in 1832 and was at this time a Conservative. He had been elected junior member for the University of Oxford in 1847 and Richard Greswell had been Chairman of his election committee. In December 1852 he made a powerful attack on Disraeli's budget and the Government fell. Lord Aberdeen was summoned by the Queen to form a new cabinet and Gladstone was made Chancellor of the Exchequer, a position which did not carry the high rank it does today. But his budget of April 1853 was extremely popular with the general public because it swept away a large number of customs duties. So the people of Denton would be very pleased to see him. At the same time, however, his budget extended legacy duty to all successions to property and, for the first time, he began to experience the hostility of the upper classes. This was to go on growing until, finally, he changed sides and became a Liberal in 1865.
[3] On June 2nd, 1866 she was married to The Hon. Robert Wellington Stapleton Cotton at St. Mary's, Bryanston Square by The Lord Bishop of London. A few years later this marriage ended in divorce. She married again, becoming Mrs. Wynne-Corrie.

80

assembled for the purpose that has now brought us together. I interpret your presence here today, my friends, in more ways than one. I think that you have intended by coming here to manifest a sentiment of respect and gratitude towards the excellent person through whose exertions and whose efforts, mainly, these schools are to be built and are to be, we trust, a foundation of blessing to your descendents through many generations – (*hear, hear*) – but, besides paying a mark of respect to him, I am confident that your presence here shows, in truth, that you have little need to be exhorted on the subject of the advantages of education. Thank God, the time has gone by when that question was an unopened question for the people of England; the time has gone by when it is necessary to argue and contend in order to convince men of the duty of multiplying the means of education. In every part of England – and most of all, perhaps, in that part we now stand, the inhabitants of which have been blessed by Providence with gifts inferior to those of no population in the world – it can be little necessary to dilate upon this subject. If, indeed, we did want a lesson upon the subject of the blessings of education, we might reflect upon the case of our more northern neighbours. We well know that that portion of our island which is called Scotland is inferior to most countries of the globe – greatly inferior to most parts of the continent of Europe – in the fertility of its soil and in the aids which a genial climate gives, for bringing the kindly products of the earth to maturity. But that country, bristling with rough and shaggy mountains – that country poor as it is comparatively in those original materials on which the first industry of man sets to work – has taken a place among nations second to no other; and even among Englishmen, Scotchmen are not found to fall behind in any gift, in the capacity for any work, or any vocation in life. (*Hear, Hear*). It was not so in former times. If we go back 300 or 400 years, they were then a nation in the rear of Europe; they are now in the front, in the van. If was ask. what is the reason of this great, this astonishing change in their relative position I believe the reason is to be found in the one great advantage they have now enjoyed for more than two centuries, in a degree beyond any other country – far beyond England – namely, this advantage, that every labouring man in Scotland had has the means of sending his children to school, where they would receive the benefits and blessings of education. (*Hear, Hear*). And the consequence of that has been, that there is an appreciation of those blessings among the people of Scotland continually growing with the enjoyment of them. (*Applause*).

"What has been said, in an evil sense, of the craving for wealth may with truth be said, in a good sense, of education – that the appetite for education grows with that on which it feeds. (*Applause*). That appetite has now sprung up among ourselves. Every man who hears me knows that in the pursuit he has to carry on, the command of knowledge is greatly available to the development of his purposes and his capacities and to the attainment of success. He knows more than this, more than that the blessing of education helps him in his art, his trade, his vocation, whatever it may be; he knows likewise that education, if it be rightly given and rightly used, helps him to fulfil those great responsibilities which rest upon him, those responsibilities which belong to him in respect of wants and needs higher than the wants and needs of the body, that it helps him to cultivate and train his mind – helps him to open out and to use the various gifts with which it has pleased Providence to endow us, whose beneficient will it was that our views, our thoughts and our desire should not be limited to the narrow scope of visible objects and to a few short years in this vale of uncertainty and trouble, but that we should pierce beyond the curtain that encloses us with the objects of sight that we should pierce beyond the bound which death affixes to our temporal existence – that what we do not see here should be the object of our cares, and that the life we are to lead in another world should be the main object of our hopes. (*Hear, Hear*). These are the subjects to which education introduces us. Those things are now well understood and there cannot be any more conclusive proof that they are understood than is afforded by the masses gathered around us today, when meeting to perform this simple, unostentatious but most important work of laying the foundation stone of schools for the township of Denton.

"There are only two other remarks which I will venture to make to you. My reverend friend, Mr. Greswell, who is the main instrument in this happy and beneficent work, has no sooner completed one beneficent work than he begins another. Is not that a lesson for us all? (*Hear, Hear*). Does not that teach us all that our motto as men must be 'Onward' – that there is nothing we can do in the world upon which we ought to rest – that our possessions, our distinctions, be they what they may, are in fact not to gloat upon, not to sleep upon – (*hear, hear*) – but as incentives to further honourable exertion – as helps to advancement in the path of duty. (*Applause*).

"One word yet. What is the work that he has consummated today? It is the consecration of a church. What is the work of which he undertakes the commencement today? It is the foundation of a school. The church is to be the symbol of spiritual truth and powers; the school is to us the symbol of a varied instruction, founded and based upon religion, – (*hear, hear*) – but likewise extended to those branches of knowledge which bear directly upon the performance of our common duties in our trades and vocations. (*Hear, hear*). And what lesson do we learn from the happy union we have seen today, between the consecration of a church and the foundation of a school? We learn this: that there is no natural opposition between the training and cultivation of the human intellect and the offering up of the soul and body of man, of all his powers, of all he can have, and all he can do, to God his Maker, from whom he has received them. On the contrary, that there is the closest and happiest harmony between the two – that he commits a profanation against God and against human nature who would attempt to disown them – that where the truths of the Christian faith are fully taught and rightly received, there will you best and most faithfully pursue the work of that temporal and secular training which is the specific object of the school. Those are then truths that we learn from the union my reverend friend has been enabled to present today between the two objects. And, gentlemen, I am sure there is not one of us who does not heartily re-echo, with all the powers of his soul, those prayers which have been offered up to heaven, that it would please the Almighty to bless this great work – to bless it in its beginning, in its continuance, I would not say its termination, for I trust it will never end. I believe, on the contrary, that every blessing which this neighbourhood derives from these schools will have within itself a multiplying power and that each generation, as it grows up to manhood, will derive from them, if they be conducted in the spirit in which they have been founded, and continually growing powers, both to discharge aright duties that belong to man upon this earth and likewise to lay up for themselves in heaven a better treasure than any that this earth can confer." (*Applause*).[1]

Three cheers were given for the Queen, for Mr. Gladstone and for the Bishop of Oxford. Then the crowd dispersed.

Stray Thoughts

In the same year that these important events took place, Horace Jackson who carried on a saddler's business in Denton, published a little paper

---

[1] *North Cheshire Herald*, October 15th, 1853. A shorthand writer would take down this speech, which is a typical example of Gladstone's tendency to become (in Disraeli's famous phrase) "inebriated with the exuberance of his own verbosity."

booklet of 36 pages (measuring 3½ inches by 6 inches) with a green cover. He called it "Stray Thoughts, a Collection of Miscellaneous Poems" and it caused a great deal of hilarity. He took himself completely seriously, but his attempts at poetry were so deplorable that most of his efforts are better consigned to limbo. Yet that's not to say all his verses are without interest. His liveliest effort is this:

LINES
Written on calling at the Robin Hood Beerhouse,
Rainsworth, between Mansfield and Southwell,
Nottinghamshire.

Here dines a poet on most wretched fare,
The worst of cheese, and muddy stinking beer;
With coarse brown bread, that's fusty, sweet and sour,
Mould bran itself from wheat could yield no flour.
Sad, unbaked, had scarce the oven seen,
Scarce fit for swine, nay e'en for swine too mean.
While thus regal'd, I sorrowing sit and heave,
The loathsome dough unto my teeth doth cleave;
I try to swallow, the sickening palate raise,
Recoiling back my craving disobeys.
Then raise the cup – why curs'd with power to smell?
And nature seems determin'd to rebel.
Thus hungry sit, the loathsome victuals lie,
I heave to view, must needs avert the eye.
Thirsty am, before me putrid beer,
An empty purse, nor work my hopes to cheer;
And footsore too, I scarcely dare to tread,
Nor know I how or where to lay my head;
With heart too proud to make my sufferings known,
To invite the sneer of each unfeeling clown.
Who envies me, such comforts may he share,
Who paints a hell on earth, behold it here.
September, 1837

One of his poems is in honour of Queen Victoria, but this does not prevent him from expressing somewhat Non-conformist views about religion and politics. Here is a broadside against employers which is certainly full of genuine feeling:

TO THE —— ——*

Written during the Stockport Strike

Shall I call you men? – I faintly will!
    Tho' sadly you disgrace that high estate, 'tis true;
By native right or accident you fill,
    And many a sorrowing parent feels it too.
Oh, shame! oh, shame! you feelingless and proud,
    Thus to pound down your fellow-creature – man –
His life's bright sunshine – sweet existence – cloud,
    And all hell's passions through his nature fan.

Shall I call it honest? – No I won't!
    To shameless purge your sacred word for gain;
And self-convinced, stand branded and abhored,
    Where dwells a spark of decency or shame.
Oh, shame! oh, shame! ye tyrant lords of toil,
    Thus to ignore that God-like noble self:
Those trusting supplicants thus faithlessly beguile,
    Whose stint existence accumulate your welath.

Shall I call you feeling? – I wish I could!
    Go render back that t–p–c– you stole;
Pinched out in morsels from the people's food,
    Life's flickering current sparkling in your bowl.
Oh, shame! oh, shame! to feast on human gore,
    Rob the poor pittance from the honest labourer's toil;
'Neath your vile feet to trample on the floor,
    And those poor supplicants without a bed the while.

Shall I call you wise? – Oh, no! oh, no!
    Nor will your children in time to come the same;
But feel the sigma your knavery o'er them throw,
    And blush to own from whom they drew their name.
Oh, shame! oh, shame! to sit on judgement's seat,
    With your broken promise and example vile;
Oh you gaunt hypocrites to bend at mercies feet,
Begirt with plunder and retain the spoil.

Though I admit their right to buy as cheap and sell as dear as they can, I assert that they ought to keep their promises.

The blank title of this poem is easy to guess – "To The Mill Owners" and it was written during the great ten per cent strike of June to August

1853. In 1848, during a depression in the cotton industry the Stockport operatives accepted a ten per cent reduction in wages on the undertaking by their employers that when trade revived it would be restored. By 1853 prosperity had returned, but the employers refused to admit any obligation to their workers. The strike lasted eight weeks, at the end of which all branches of the cotton trade got their ten per cent, except the weavers who accepted five.

Being a saddler, it comes as no surprise to find him writing about his craft. He imagines a saddle talking to him as Parr Greswell had the old yew tree.

THE OLD PILLION'S PETITION
on being converted into a milk-saddle.

Hold, saddler, hold! nor thus my entails tear,
But hear my tale and pitying drop a tear;
O thou immortal, some other form go try,
Go change thy nature, and suffering, still not die;
Bear thou this havoc dissected and deranged,
Thy form new-model'd, and thy function changed;
Thy joints untendoned, or thy limbs thus spread,
Thy entails drawn to serve the swine for bed.
This have I borne, yea, and much more,
This have I borne, two separate times before;*
And now a third, that's far more cruel still,
Sent to your butchers, again to do your will.
Cut, slash, and tear, without the least restraint,
Deaf to each cry, unheeding each complaint;
Slash my old course with many a hideous gore,
Rummage my bowels and turn them o'er and o'er;
Take part out, extend my contracted maw,
And stuff me full of rotten flocks and straw,
Beat my old sides, and make my bones to crack,
And send me forth with hunches on my back;
Then fix vile hooks, a servile load to bear,
To cheat mankind without restraint or care.
A spurious mixture simple town-folks buy
For genuine milk, though full one-third's alloy.
I who have borne with such becoming pride,
The modest virgin or the blushing bride;
Mounted behind her heart's accepted lord I've borne

The blushing virgin, smiling as the morn,
Swift to Hymen's then in my youth and prime,
Bearing a load had feelings most sublime.
The joyous feelings virgin ever knew
Bound with each pulse, and through each artery flew
Fraught tim'rous mixture, trem'lous hopeful fear,
Sweet agitation – sublimest hope severe –
Almost too much for human heart to feel,
The joyous cup stands up to convex fill.
One trifling jar, the glorious draught is shed,
Pangs chilling fear, and feels a heart of lead.
But now no more these vain regrets I'll wail,
Doom'd to the menial, and drudgeries entail;
I'll bear betimes the cheerless orphan boy,
And feel delighted when I give him joy;
To rest his toil I'll lend my willing aid,
Nor grieving thence at this ignoble trade.

Having previously been converted into a women's, and then into a man's saddle.

He may have been a good saddler, but he certainly was no poet. He knew this, yet still enjoyed publishing his 'thoughts' and probably was not in the least surprised when some of his readers simply could not resist a joke at his expense. In November, the following advertisement appeared in the *Hyde Gazette:*—

" 'Tis pleasant sure, to see one's name in print,
A book's a book, although there's nothing in't."
"Lost a few days ago, the STRAY THOUGHTS of a Denton Poet and Hyde Saddler. Whosoever has found the same, on restoring them to their owner, shall be rewarded with an a-cross-stick."

This last sentence needs explanation. In the booklet, Jackson had written acrostic poems on the names of three of his friends – Thomas Harrison, William Peacock[1] and Zachariah Peacock. Although intended as compliments they are of such poor quality that the three gentlemen concerned would certainly have gladly done without them! The anonymous advertisers are warning people not to risk suffering a similar fate by be-friending poor Horace!

A modern newspaper editor would not accept such an advertisement but in the mid-nineteenth century libel laws were not as strict as they are today. Sometimes really insulting notices appeared on the front page of

[1] One of the First Churchwardens of Christ Church and Hat Master.

newspapers. Here is an excellent example from *The Ashton Standard* of September 27th, 1862:

"There is a Clergyman near Ashton-under-Lyne who is fond of Domineering, for whom if any person will find a better living he may not only have the Minister, but something very handsome with him.

The Parson is GREEN and his head is WOOD."

This refers to The Revd. J. H. Greenwood, incumbent of St. John's, Hurst. It contains real malice and reminds us that clergy were not always treated with respect in those days.

But to return to Horace Jackson; let him have the last word. He put this little postscript at the end of his booklet:

"As Poet I know, I must rank rather low.
As Saddler command some respect;
But takes me as a Poet and Saddler too,
As good as you well can expect."

A Life at One Living

By now William Parr Greswell was old and feeble. His wife Anne had died on May 13th, 1841 and he had no daughter to comfort him in old age. Charles, the surgeon, had died on May 8th, 1844. Only four of the nine children outlived their father. When J(ohn) P(ollit) wrote his article for the *Strines Journal* in 1853, Edward was living with is father and had a fine reputation amongst the poor of Denton for his generosity to them. P(ollit) was obviously moved and impressed by the sight of the old man. "Mr. Greswell is now in the 88th year of his age and as may naturally be expected is very feeble. The greater part of his life has been spent in arduous study. He is the author of several works, one on the early Parisian typographers. He is alike distinguished for his learning and simplicity; he is entirely without ostentation and is an honour to the village in which he lives."[1]

In June 1853 he was photographed by Mr. Joseph Sidebotham of Apethorn House, Hyde, one of his former pupils. The picture shows him in the homely fustian and brown gaiters he wore on week-days. On Sundays his dress was always the scrupulously-fine broad-cloth with the somewhat long frock coat and great white neck-cloth. Always he wore the eighteenth century shovel or "Dr. Syntax" hat. He preached in a black academic gown with white bands, but wore a white surplice when administering the scraments.[2]

[1] *Strines Journal*, October 1853, page 266. In fact, Parr Greswell had written *Two* books on the Parisian Typographers.
[2] Middleton: page 67, column 2.

Towards the end of 1853 he finally resigned the living and out of compliment to him the Bishop, Dr. Lee attended at Denton chapel to receive his resignation. Walter Nicol, his faithful curate, was given the chapelry and in the Baptism Register on January 1st, 1854 signs himself – Walter Nicol, M.A., Incumbent.

Eleven days later Parr Greswell died. The Bishop of Manchester once again came out to Denton to conduct the funeral service, the Revd. Walter Nicol preaching the sermon. Then the body was laid to rest in the family grave by the east gate. Undoubtedly he was the greatest man Denton saw in both the eighteenth and nineteenth centuries, but there are no fine words on this tombstone. It only records one bare and simple fact:—

WILLIAM PARR GRESWELL
for 63 years Minister of the Adjoining Chapel.

CHAPTER FOUR

THE FIRST RECTOR

ON FRIDAY, June 16th, 1854, *The London Gazette* announced that the district chapelry of Denton had become the District of Saint Lawrence, Denton by order of the Queen's Most Excellent Majesty in Council. In effect this established the parish that we know today and Incumbents were permitted to call themselves Rectors.

The Right Reverend James Prince, first Bishop of the new diocese of Manchester (which had been created in 1847) allowed Walter Nicol to become the first Rector. He had proved a wonderful strength to Parr Greswell in his old age and no doubt the parishioners were pleased that the assistant curate who had done nearly all the work during the last five years should be acknowledged in this way.

The Rev. Walter Nicol,
Rector, 1853-1869.

Marriages Again

On April 14th, 1854, the people of Denton saw a wedding at the old church. It was the first one to be held there since 1754, when the Government had restricted the number of churches at which marriages could be solemnized because too many young couples were getting married surreptitiously without their parents consent. And something new had happened since 1754. Couples were now required to sign their names and two witnesses had to sign with them. Needless to say, the register abounds with crosses throughout the fifties, sixties and seventies. It is only in the eighties that such marks became uncommon. For example, in 1854 and 1855 there were twelve marriages but only three at which all four signatories could write their names and one of them is very touching. Charles Lowe, a collier of thirty-five years struggles to sign his name at his wedding on June 4th, 1855. He succeeds – but only just! his writing is big and spidery and he misses the R out of Charles! Of the 48 people called on to sign (12 couples and 24 witnesses) fifteen had to make a cross. The first really "big" wedding seems to have been the one on June 18th, 1857, when George Waterloo Pennington Sparrow, Surgeon to the Sixtieth Rifles, married Elizabeth Eleanor Pickering, who was a surgeon's daughter. It must have been a splendid Victorian scene!

The First Rectory

Wilton House had been lent to Parr Greswell for as long as he lived, but when he died it reverted to the Earl of Wilton. The reason for this was that at the end of the eighteenth century the Wardens and Fellows of Manchester parish church (now the Cathedral) had claimed the rights of patronage in Denton. The Earl, determined to resist such a claim, decided that he would not give a parsonage to the chapelry lest it should be claimed by the

Photograph by David Walker
The Old Rectory (front view) Vaudrey Lane, September 1968.

Wardens and Fellows. He would build a house which he undoubtedly owned and *lend* it to the Greswell family. The arrangement worked well enough until Mr. Nicol was inducted as Rector. A Rector must have a Rectory.

As usual, Richard came to the rescue. He reminded the Earl that his grandfather (the first Earl of Wilton) had intended to build a parsonage that would belong to the parish. Lord Wilton accordingly gave £500 and this was augmented by grants of £200 from Queen Anne's Bounty and £50 from the Manchester Diocesan Church Building Society. Mr. David Shaw Clayton gave the site at the top of Vaudrey Lane and Richard Greswell then began to build a large stone rectory standing in its own grounds.[1] When completed the cost totalled £1,000 and it is probable that Richard, Edward and their friends supplied the other £250.

Into this Rectory Walter and Rebecca Nicol moved with their infant son William Herbert, who had been born to them in 1854. Another boy, Walter Morris was added to the family in 1857. Their father baptized them both himself in church. Nothing remains of the house today. It was demolished in 1970 and Rectory Close stands over the site.

In the Nottingham Castle

Some of the inhabitants of Denton and Haughton wanted to show their gratitude to Richard Greswell for all he had done, so they called a meeting at the Nottingham Castle,[2] appointed a committee and set about the task of collecting money. One thousand, one hundred and seven people subscribed amounts varying from five shillings to a single penny. £70 were raised and two silver trays purchased. On one was engraved a picture of Denton Chapel and on the other Christ Church. William Peacock presented them to Richard on Saturday, October 6th, 1854, "before a respectable audience"[3] at a tea in Christ Church Schoolroom. Mr. Greswell, greatly appreciating this token of respect and affection, took the trays back to Oxford, where he was tutor at Worcester College.

The Scholars' Walk and Treat

The new day school – St. Lawrence's, Stockport Road – was ready by the middle of 1855. The Sunday School committee spent £5.8.0. on two clocks. They paid a joiner one shilling to fit in a Sunday School cupboard and Moses Hardy, the sexton, was given sixpence for helping to bring

[1] Middleton: page 53.
[2] Foolishly re-named the Tollpoint in 1973.
[3] Wainwright Manuscript (His phrase).

books from the old school near the church. It's in this same year that the Treasurer's account mentions Whit Friday for the first time. The hymn papers cost four shillings and sixpence. We can be certain, however, that the Walks would have begun many years earlier and by 1855 they must have been large and impressive.

Whit Friday was the Friday *AFTER* Whit Sunday. It was widely used for walks and processions, followed by sports and games in the afternoon. Take, for example, Ashton Methodist Sunday School in the early years of the century. "In common with other South Lancashire schools, the teachers and scholars walked in procession on Whit Friday, the four schools in order of seniority. Afterwards, there were buns and home brewed beer – half a glass for the children and a full glass for the teachers."[1]

St. Lawrence's Sunday School was led by a band and carried a banner with a picture of the old church on it. In 1855 they consumed 330 tuppeny cakes and each had a drink of milk. The very next year they order a thousand buns costing £7.5.10. and pay Mr. Lowe three shlliings for taking forms to the field. In 1867 they spend twelve and eightpence on ropes, balloons and balls for the sports and games. From the middle of the nineteenth century to the first decade of the twentieth century Sunday Schools grew prodigiously, enjoying unprecedented success and immense influence. This was the time of the Young Men's and Young Ladies' Classes, consisting of adults who went to Sunday School all their lives. Many of them hardly ever went to a church service – Sunday School *was* their church and round it all their social activities centred. And Whit Friday was their day. It was the day on which the Sunday School celebrated its own success and demonstrated it with pride to the populace at large.

St. Lawrence's Cricket Club

Early in 1857 all the Sunday Schools in Denton and Haughton canvassed the townships for more members.[2] They were growing in strength and could offer such inducements to young people as lending libraries, sewing circles, singing classes and sporting activities. St. Lawrence's took a particularly adventurous step on July 6th, 1857, when it held a meeting to establish a Cricket Club. To join you had to be a member of the Sunday School or a pew-holder in church and the subscription was quite high – sixpence per month. This reminds us that the Club was not for children but adults, nevertheless, they had to maintain active membership or face expulsion. The rules were strict and deserve to be quoted in full:

[1] E. A. Rose: *Methodism in Ashton-under-Lyne* 2: (1969), page 16.
[2] *Ashton Reporter:* 4th April, 1857.

94

DENTON OLD CHURCH
SUNDAY SCHOOLS.

A NIGHT WITH

The Renowned Oldham Ventriloquist,

MR. MELLOR.

On Monday Evening, November 29th, 1869,

THE ABOVE GENTLEMAN

Will Illustrate the Polyphonic Art

BY HIS

GREAT LAUGHABLE

ENTERTAINMENT.

PROGRAMME.

Glee .... Messrs. J. B. Cooke, E. Hartley, and M. Arrowsmith
Song ....

VENTRILOQUISM......Imitations of Men, Women, and Children at various
distances ; Watchman and his Dog ; Echo of Whistle, &c......Mr. MELLOR

Dialogue .... By Teachers and Scholars

VENTRILOQUISM......Imitation of Farm Yard : Barking of Dogs; entering
of a Pigsty, &c., &c. ....Mr. MELLOR

Song ....
Glee ....

"God save the Queen."

Doors open at a Quarter past Seven, to commence at a Quarter to Eight precisely.

ADMISSION : FRONT SEATS 6D., BACK SEATS 3D. ; A FEW RESERVED SEATS 1S.

Tickets may be had from any of the Teachers, or at the Door.

J. Higham & Co., Printers, Hamnet Street, Market Place,

RULES

1. That this society be called "The St. Lawrence's Cricket Club".
2. The society shall have for its government a president, secretary and four stewards (five of whom may form a quorum), the same to be elected quarterly, from the body of the members.
3. The president shall attend and preside over all meetings of this club, to preserve regularity and order and inflict the fines in cases required by the rules.
4. The treasurer shall hold all monies belonging to the club, for which he shall give security at any time (if required). He shall keep a book with all the receipts and payments, copied from the secretary's book, nor shall he pay or settle account unless the secretary's initials are attached, to prove its correctness.
5. The secretary shall keep a clear and correct account of all the affairs and proceedings of this club, and explain and balance the same when required; he shall also examine and attach his initials or signature to all bills or accounts before they are paid by the treasurer.
6. The stewards shall keep all the implements belonging to this club in good order and attend with the secretary to receive contributions.
7. Any person being a teacher or scholar of the St. Lawrence's schools or a seat-holder of the church connected therewith, – and not being a person who has left the club in arrears previously – may become a member, after having been proposed and approved by a majority of actual members[1] and have paid up all subscriptions from the closing day of the season next previous, when his name shall be duly inscribed in the secretary's book.
8. That the subscription be sixpence per month, the committee having the power to increase or reduce the amount, according to the state of the funds.
9. Any member who shall receive a donation, gift, subscription, contribution, etc. shall deliver up the same at the first monthly meeting next succeeding; in case of default or neglect he shall be fined or reprimanded, at the discretion of the committee.
10. A box with a strong lock and two keys shall be provided, in which shall be kept all the tools, implements and other property of this club; one key to be deposited with the secretary and the other with the president.

[1] Like all other Cricket Clubs, St. Lawrence's was exclusive. To be allowed to join it would be a sign of social acceptability.

11. That no fewer than three of the members be allowed to remove for play or otherwise, except it be a member who is in another club and wishes to play with any particular bat (in which case he shall obtain the special permission of the committee), for which he shall be responsible and shall repair any loss or damage it may sustain, according to the discretion of the committee.

12. Any member who shall let his contribution run more than two months in arrear shall be fined one penny per month; nor shall he be allowed to play, unless he give satisfactory reasons to the secretary and treasurer, until he pay up the same; but if he neglect to pay in three months, notice shall be given him by the secretary; and if not paid up by the monthly meeting next succeeding, he shall cease to be a member of this club; nor shall he again be admitted, until he shall have paid up all fines and arrears, in addition to the demands of rule 7.

13. The committee shall meet in the school room every four weeks at eight p.m. for the purpose of receiving contributions, etc. and to transact any business the club may have in hand; and any officer for the time being not in attendance at half-past eight p.m. shall be fined twopence; and if not there by nine p.m. he shall be fined threepence for such neglect.

14. There shall be a quarterly general meeting of the members for the election of fresh officers and to transact any other business which may be laid before them; such general meeting to be notified to the members at least a week before by the secretary. Any member who shall not be in attendance by half-past eight p.m. shall be fined twopence; if absent at nine he shall be fined threepence for such neglect, unless he send a satisfactory reason, such reason to be considered by the committee.

15. Any member found guilty of swearing or using indecent language, at any of the meetings of this club or in the cricket field shall be fined one penny for each offence.

16. Any member behaving disorderly at any of the meetings of this club shall be called to by the president to desist, if he refuse, he shall be fined twopence for the first offence, fourpence for the second and eight-pence for each offence afterwards during the same evening.

17. The Committee shall be empowered to deal with any unforeseen event which may occur and they may make such bye-laws as they think proper, provided they do not counteract these general laws.

18. A quarterly report of the proceedings of this club shall be read aloud by the retiring secretary at the quarterly general meeting.

19. Any member who has any grievance or cause to complain shall attend at the committee meeting and state his complaint which shall be considered by the committee; and if the decision of the committee do not satisfy him, he shall have the right of appeal to the next general meeting whose decision shall be final.

20. All disputes which may arise during playing shall be decided by the Umpire, who shall be provided with the latest published rules of the Marylebone Club.

21. This club shall not be broken up so long as there are twelve persons who are members in accordance with rule 12; but if the number of members be reduced to less than twelve, then the remaining members may close up the club altogether if they think proper, when the cash, implements and all perquisites belonging to the club, shall be equally divided amongst them or be disposed of in any other way they may think proper.

22. If any member wilfully and maliciously strike another member, either in the field or at a meeting of this club, he shall be fined one shilling for each offence nor shall be allowed to play again until the fine is paid.

23. Any member refusing to serve in office after having been duly elected by a majority of the members, shall be fined sixpence unless he has officiated during the three months previous.

24. If any member of this club shall discontinue his attendance at the school for more than three weeks successively without giving a sufficient reason, he shall be considered as having left the school; and if he do not hold a seat in the church, he shall be expelled the club, in order that the privileges may be insured and reserved.

BYE-LAWS

1. Every person who shall become a member of this club shall be presented with a printed copy of the rules.

2. Any member who shall thrown down a bat when out shall be fined one penny for such offence.

3. Any member who shall create a disturbance or cause an ill feeling to exist amongst the members, by speaking of or against the proceedings of this club, except at a meeting of the committee or a general meeting shall be fined threepence for such offence.

4. Any member may be allowed the privilege of introducing a friend on the field of play, if such member be not in arrears.[1]

[1] I am very grateful to Mr. Frank Heaton for supplying me with these rules.

These were rough times and behaviour was obviously such a problem that the rules harp obsessively on complaints, reprimands, fines and expulsion. They were published in a little six page booklet printed in 1858 and the earliest report of the club's activities in the newspapers is a report on the match played on June 19th of that year. Does this mean that the club did not manage to organise itself for play during the 1857 season? Possibly so – and judging by the score they were very inexperienced. They lost to Denton Victoria, only scoring 23 runs in their first innings against Victoria's 73. They were put in to bat again, but still only made 29. So Victoria won by an innings and 21 runs. It must have been a good day for bowlers![1]

"I Will Build You a School"

Walter Nicol was an extremely hard-working man. Although the creation of the parish of Christ Church reduced the number of baptisms, weddings and funerals he had to take, there was still a great deal of work to do and he never had a curate.

Conscious of the fact that Haughton Green was an outlying part of his parish in which Primitive Methodists were at work, he not only encuraged the Sunday School at the Bay Horse Inn which lay-folk were running, but also obtained a bishop's licence to hold Sunday evening "lectures" in the same club room.[2] Mr. Nicol would be free to go to Haughton Green on a Sunday evening because St. Lawrence's would still be having its two services, morning and afternoon, during daylight hours. Evening lectures, which had started in some parishes during the 1840's, were almost like a Free Church service and a Bible Class rolled into one. They catered for the uneducated and their simple form made them very popular. Meeting a crying need, they helped to foster the growing increase in church and chapel attendance which was already discernable throughout the country as a whole.

The inhabitants of Haughton Green undoubtedly felt neglected. They started a day school in a cottage which soon proved too small so Mr. James Walton allowed it to be held in his mill in Haughton Dale. This mill, built about 1790, to spin cotton, stood on the river at the bottom of Meadow Lane. Mr. Walton had bought it from the Sidebotham family and in 1853 he extended it considerably. The new part was a three storey building, consisting of cast-iron units with larger windows of thick glass and in it Mr. Walton set up machinery for manufacturing carding wire by

[1] *Ashton Reporter*, June 26th, 158.
[2] Middleton: page 77.

means of a process he had invented. He had already erected a large works of some kind in Manchester in 1846 and was well on the way to becoming an immensely rich industrialist. Middleton says that at the time of his death in 1883 Haughton Dale Wireworks "was probably the largest works of its kind in the world."[1]

The school in the factory was a success, but the children had to try to concentrate against the background noise of machinery. It soon became clear that what was needed was a proper, purpose-built school. The Sunday School Committee decided to take action. They approached Mr. Walton with the request that he should head the subscription list. He did so by writing across it the words, "I will build you a school."[2] It was one of those magnificent gestures of which Victorian philanthropists were so proud! And the result was equally striking. Taking some of those cast iron units with thick glass windows, he built "The Iron School" in 1858. It was an exceedingly attractive little building, standing on the site of the present Sunnyside Club and had it survived it would certainly be scheduled as a monument of historic interest. Unfortunately, it was pulled down in 1905 as the Lancashire Education authorities were not satisfied with it. But in 1858 the Iron School served as a day school, a Sunday School, an institute for leisure activities and a church in which evening services were held.

The Iron School.

[1] Middleton: page 158. Walton leased the Haughton Dale Cotton Mill to Messrs. Wood & Co. It closed in May, 1873 (*Ashton Reporter*, May 10th, 1873). The Wireworks closed in March, 1903.
[2] Middleton: page 77.

The 1859 Restoration

In September 1859 St. Lawrence's church was closed to allow workmen to completely re-order the interior. Mr. Samuel Bramhall, a well-known builder and contractor from Manchester, was entrusted with this important work. It took him until Christmas and services were held in St. Lawrence's school whilst the re-fitting was in progress.

What happened was extremely important for it altered the character of the interior decisively and we cannot read the account of it without feeling sad.[1]

When John Angier was minister, (1632–1677), a new oak pulpit and prayer desk were given to the chapel in 1659. This pulpit stood against the north wall, half-way down, in front of the wooden pillar which today bears the little brass shield of the Shawcross bequest. The nave, on either side of the centre aisle, was full of all kinds of seats, stalls, forms and box pews, put there by the families which owned them and we can be certain that it would all look very disorderly.

In 1786 the Denton people decided to re-pew the north side, "the seats, stalls and forms therein having by length of time become old, ruinous and decayed."[2] The people of Haughton followed suit by applying for a faculty to re-pew the south side. In place of the old seats, stalls and forms they wished "to erect new, handsome and convenient seats or pews and also to take in from the middle aisle twenty-two inches or thereabouts in order to make the said new erection more regular and uniform."[3]

To decide to do something is one thing; to carry it out is another and it appears from the evidence available that only the Haughtonians fulfilled their intentions. The south side was re-pewed but not the north. The Bishop's Register in the Chester Record Office only contains the faculty to re-pew the south side. The north side citation which Middleton quotes on page 39 did not succeed in producing a faculty.[4] A passage in Joel Wainwright's letter to the Reverend W. Greswell, Rector of Doddington, Somerset, describes this strange state of affairs: "Many years elapsed before Dentonians followed the example of their Haughtonian neighbours in pewing the north side of the edifice, consequently the sittings on the north side were derisively termed the "Owd bed stocks" where the worshippers' feet were comfortably immersed in rushes. I do not remember the rushes

---

[1] Samuel Hadfield saw it all. His account is in the *Ashton Standard* of September 27th, 1862.

[2] Middleton: page 39. Citation of October 6th, 1768.

[3] Faculty of January 5th, 1769. Cheshire Record Office.

[4] A Citation is an announcement rather like Banns of Marriage. It states an *intention* to do something and calls for objections to it. If there are no objections a faculty is issued and the work proceeds. Middleton should not have assumed that the re-pewing was done when he had only seen a citation. Did a pew-holder raise an objection and prevent the proposed work?

but I can well recollect that the floor in the pews was simply the bare earth or soil under the seats, there being a loose board or two for the feet. The boards were various shapes and not made to fit."[1]

When Booker visited the church in 1854 he was not impressed by the pews. He could see that they were not as old as the pulpit. But his attention was caught by three or four box-pews on the north side of the little chancel. Some of these bore the arms of the Hyde family and might well have been sixteenth century. How good it would be if we still had them today! But we don't! The axe was about to fall! Mr. Nicol and his wardens considered that the pews were in such a sad state of dilapidation that Mr. Bramhall was ordered to rip out all the internal fittings. Angier's pulpit and the box-pews were "reverently consumed by fire!" In their place new, low-backed pews of red deal – the ones we have today – were installed, all facing east and a new pulpit was placed on the north side of the chancel, balanced by a lectern-cum-prayer desk on the south. You can see them in the photograph on page 00 which was taken sometime between 1862 and 1872. No doubt this would enable the church to hold more people, but it was no longer the church which Parr Greswell had known. And what a loss to us! Today, we must go to St. Michael's, Ashton-under-Lyne to see a pulpit in the old position and box-pews around it.

The Interior after the 1859 Restoration.

The congregation, however, were well pleased with the new rented pews, which they used for the first time on Sunday, December 18th. They had a

[1] Wainwright Manuscript, 1896.

memorable day. The Reverend J. H. Marsden, B.D., Canon of Manchester and Rector of Great Oakley, Essex, was the special preacher in the morning and the Reverend C. Marshall, M.D., Rector of Harpurhey in the afternoon.

The Rector in Court

John Cotteral (or Cottril) the old sexton, had died in March 1831, having filled the post for 30 years. He was 79 and his wife Nancy had died a few weeks before him in January at the age of 80. Hadfield told Middleton[1] that many years later her gravestone turned up in the kitchen of The Chapelhouse during alterations. When workmen turned it over it read:—

1817

Nancy Cottril

"May the wings of liberty never be clipped."

It could not have been her gravestone, but it does look like a lintel stone, that is, an inscription set over a cottage doorway. It does not actually say she had died and "May the wings of liberty never be clipped" is a political sentiment of a kind rarely, if ever, found on a tombstone. This stone was either taken from the cottage doorway where she had lived or it refers to another Nancy Cottril altogether.

Very probably the man chosen to succeed Cottril was Moses Hardy. He had been born in 1791 and one day he asked if he could see the entry of his baptism in the parish register. When the page was found he was somewhat dismayed. He had been recorded as a girl – Elizabeth![2] Parr Greswell crossed it out and wrote, "N.B. This ought to be Moses."

As sexton he was as much a frequenter of the Chapelhouse as his predecessors. Usually, as we can see from the registers, there were three or four graves to be dug or re-opened each week, but occasionally things went slack. One day when Moses was sat in The Chapelhouse his wife burst in and exclaimed with indignation: "You ought ot be ashamed of yourself – sitting there like that when you've never buried a single living soul all this week!"[3] And what did Moses look like? By the oddest quirk of history his photograph has survived! For we can be fairly certain that the cheerful man standing next to the South-east door in the photograph on page 104 is Moses Hardy. He was around when Joseph Sidebottom came to photograph the old chapel in May 1853.

[1] Middleton: page 55.
[2] May 18th, 1791.
[3] Middleton: page 140.

Moses Hardy at the Chapel Door.

In February 1860, Moses had a sharp disagreement with the Rector. We don't know what it was about, but it resulted in his dismissal. He was sixty-nine at the time and to lose one's job in days when there was no old age pension was serious. But Moses had a mentally sub-normal boy who worked at the Rectory, so he immediately kept him at home. This lad, John, was in fact thirty-seven, but so simple that everyone looked upon him as a child. His main work was pulling Mrs. Nicol around the village in a bath carriage, because she had unfortunately become a permanent invalid.

Moses was convinced that the Nicols had withheld wages from his boy, so he took the Rector to Court claiming £8.10.8d. The account of the case in a local newspaper[1] is a very full one, giving us a clear picture of the

[1] Possibly the *North Cheshire Herald*. The cutting is pasted into a scrap book in the possession of Denton Public Library.

situation. Witnesses called by Moses Hardy described the lad's work in detail. It was, said one, "horse-work for the small pittance of the weekly sum named." (One shilling and eightpence per week!) He drew Mrs. Nicol about in a bath carriage almost daily and fetched water and milk for the use of the family. Mr. Lees, a farmer, said he had seen him getting water for which he had to go two hundred yards and it was very hard work. In the course of questioning, the Court learnt that sometimes John pulled the bath carriage as far as Stockport, but Mr. Nicol "rendered the boy aid."

In their defence The Reverend and Mrs. Nicol said that there had never been any agreement about wages for the lad, but they gave him all his meals except breakfast and kept him in clothes. Mrs. Nicol admitted that she had kept back £2.12.0. due to him with which "she intended to buy him outer clothes." It was stressed that he couldn't be employed in any normal job as he was too sub-normal. He would even go to a friend's house for a pinch of snuff, leaving Mrs. Nicol in the road! "He was a very innocent person."

The Court found against the Nicols. They were ordered to pay £2.12.0. to Moses Hardy and the costs of the case. They had had a servant at a scandalously low cost to themselves and the Court realised this. Whether poor John found any other employment we don't know, but five years later Moses died and was buried by Walter Nicol on July 16th, 1865 in the yard in which he had dug so many graves for others.

Alpha Mill – and Baxendale's Band

The Great Cotton panic of 1861 did not directly affect Denton, but unemployment was still a problem as the hatting industry had never really recovered from the depression of the 1840's. For this reason the Earl of Wilton persuaded Mr. Thomas Baxendale to introduce the cotton trade into Denton and as an inducement he gave him the land at the top of Taylor Lane on which to build Alpha Mill – so called because it was the first cotton mill in the town.[1] Mr. Baxendale was a generous member of the United Methodist Church and also the founder and patron of a brass band.[2] It began its life in 1859 and when Alpha Mill was completed in 1862 set up its headquarters there, but after a short time moved to a room behind the Bowling Green Inn. Nevertheless, for years it continued to be known as "Baxendale's Band" and it attained increasingly high standards of performance under its conductor, Mr. Whittam Smith. As time went by it changed its name to "Denton Original Band" and won many competitions.

[1] Mr. Walton's Mill was in Haughton.
[2] Middleton: page 135.

The crowning triumph came in 1900 when it won the thousand-guinea cup at the Crystal Palace.[1]

Cheering though the band must have been, the employment offered by Alpha Mill was more so. An article in the *North Cheshire Herald* of 1865 states that the condition of the felt bodymakers of Denton then "had no parallel even in the handloom weavers of yore, who were compelled to fly to steam looms for a paltry pittance." The writer rejoiced over Alpha Mill and added that as hatting seemed doomed, Denton might be proud that the cotton trade had been introduced to find employment for the people.[2]

The 1862 Restoration

Although the church had been re-pewed and re-ordered, the exterior was still in a serious state of dilapidation, so in 1862 a Mr. Clay of Manchester was contracted and his men set to work. Samuel Hadfield went to see what they were doing and here is his account,[3] published in 1864.

"Some 16 months ago, hearing that Denton Old Chapel was undergoing a thorough external repair and that most of the cement was stripped off and the original structure laid naked and exposed to view, we ventured to avail ourselves of the opportunity of seeing the timber work as the carpenters originally placed it.

"On a low footing or basement of stone was reared a strong framework of oak timber, consisting of upright timbers intersected by three heights of horizontal beams, extending the length of the structure. The lower frames were again subdivided by perpendicular legs, leaving only a few inches space between them for the purpose of filling in with raddling and daub – now replaced by bricks and mortar, though some of the daub remaining showed a liberal allowance of chopped straw or rushes. The upper panes are strengthened by a series of diagonal or bracing ribs and also contain all the window lights, one only excepted[4] and that near what, if ancient, we consider to have been the priest's entrance originally.

"The drippings from the eaves, in the absence of gutters and spouts, have fallen beside the basement and run into the foundations, owing to the want of soughs and drains. Good foundations have been

[1] Middleton: page 146.
[2] Middleton: page 14. Alpha Mill was burnt down on Thursday, April 22nd, 1915.
[3] *North Cheshire Herald*, March 5th, 1864.
[4] Wrong! There were 4 windows below the mid-way horizontal beam. Hadfield, usually so accurate, is possibly speaking of the little window by the south-east door which disappeared at the enlargement, but three others remain to this day; two at the north-west corner where the hymn books are kept and one by the Wardens' pew.

secured and in one place besides the southern entrance door, near the western end, the workmen had to go 6 ft. 2 in. deeper than their predecessors of three centuries and a quarter ago. The stay-bolts or rods have been shortened, the structure drawn in and underwalled, the plaster removed, timber casing affixed and then painted to represent the framework in a style more in accordance with truth than was formerly the case. During the repairing the box or side chapel, erected on the north side in 1676 by Mr. Hyde has disappeared altogether in order to make way for a lumber-room."

Robert Hyde's Strange "Pew"

From the above account it is clear that the wooden planking along the south side of the church was put on as weather boarding in this restoraton. It spoils the effect, making a genuine tudor church look mock-tudor! It's a disappointment to see the black beams painted on planking. But this is nothing compared to the disappointment we feel when we realise what the removal of Robert Hyde's pew means.

In November 1676 Robert Hyde of Hyde Hall, Denton was seventy-two and hard of hearing. He had two forms within the chapel but could not hear Mr. Angier when he read, prayed and preached. In order to get nearer to him he sent his men to knock a hole in the chapel wall as near to the pulpit as they could get. The pulpit, which stood in the middle of the north side, was a high one, so the workmen erected a little "chapel", only four feet square, standing on timber stilts and fixed to the outside wall. It can be seen in the beautiful watercolour painted by Samuel Sidley some time between 1854 and 1862, which now hangs in church.[1]

Mr. Hyde had acted without a faculty or any authority whatever. He angered other leading members of the congregation and local gentry with rights in the chapel, but nevertheless the pew on stilts remained. In Parr Greswell's day some of the boys who attended his little grammar school had to sit in it on Sunday mornings, so that he could keep a sharp eye on th em. It was proably a very draughty little place and its "aperature", (as Hadfield calls it) was covered by a curtain. He tells us that when it was dismantled in 1862 the aperature was replaced by a window,[2] but this must also be wrong as the outline of the aperture can still be seen in the plaster to the right of the Shawcross pillar. In the little lumber-room underneath a heating apparatus was installed.[3] Was this the first heating the church had ever had ?

[1] The whole story is told at length by Middleton: pages 48–49.
[2] Samuel Hadfield: *Ashton Standard*, September 27th, 1862.
[3] *Ashton Standard*, September 27th, 1862.

Probably not. In Heywood's "Life of Angier" there's a passing reference to the fact that when Angier came out of the pulpit in his later years he put a warmed scarlet cloth on his chest to stop himself catching cold. He was very subject to catch cold after preaching as the effort made him perspire.[1] But where did he warm the cloth? Was there some sort of open brazier in the chapel?

So perished Robert Hyde's unique old "pew." It was criminal to destroy it and if we had it today our church would be celebrated for it. But the Dentonians of those days wanted a modern Victorian parish church and the alterations pleased them. They kept the top of the old back of the ancient wardens' pew, set it into the wall behind the new one and screwed on to it a little square metal plate bearing the following inscription:—

This church
was renewed and thoroughly
RESTORED
by the
Landowners & Congregation

A.D. 1862

Walter Nicol M.A. Rector

John Gould	Wardens	John Bradbury	Sidesmen
John Bentley		Peter Rothwell	

"And we will not forsake the house of our God"
Nehemiah X, 39.

The Market Square

In the same year, 1862, the churchwardens John Gould and John Bentley, called a meeting of ratepayers to consider buying a plot of land for a market square.[2] It was a noisy meeting with plenty of objectors to the idea, but the wardens got their way and on October 10th, 1863, the first sod was cut amid great rejoicing. It was John Bentley himself (he was also a magistrate), who cut the first turf. He "took off his coat, rolled up his shirt sleeves and handled the spade in a manner that would have done credit to an experienced navvy. He delved sod after sod until he had filled his barrow, which he wheeled along the plank and then tipped up."[3] There followed a monster bonfire and three barrels of ale were consumed.

[1] Heywood: page 38.
[2] *Ashton Standard*, July 12th, 1862.
[3] Middleton: quoting a newspaper, page 14.

St. Lawrence's Church by Samuel Sidley, showing Robert Hyde's "Pew".
Photograph by David Walker.

These celebrations were all very well, provided ratepayers put firmly out of their minds the uncomfortable fact that they had failed to keep the Manchester to Hyde turnpike road in repair. Its trustees brought an action against Denton and it was heard at the Liverpool Assizes in 1863. The judge imposed a fine of £1,000, but delayed the levying of his order to give the town a chance to repair the road. Nothing, however, was done, so on April 2nd, 1864, the judge ordered the fine to be paid and added a further £467, which was to be spent on repairs immediately.[1]

The Churchyard is Enlarged

Tradition says that the first burial in the chapel graveyard was that of John Angier's first wife in 1642. Before that date corpses were carried to Ashton, Stockport or Manchester parish churches. Certainly, the chapel yard was very small indeed until the nineteenth century. It was enlarged by Richard Greswell in 1853 on the eastern side, when the original parsonage was demolished, but the really important enlargement was in 1867. The old school by the lych-gate was demolished in that year, (it had been used as a machine shop since 1855) and a faculty was obtained to add on 2,103

[1] Middleton: page 15.

square yards – the long piece from the north side of the church up to Cooke Street.

The plan also indicated that a new street was to be made to the west of the church. We know it as Market Street, but the original proposal was that it should be called Sidney Street. It was to go straight through the row of four cottages which stood close to the west end of the church, but they were still not demolished by the time the church was enlarged. We know this because the end cottage, at one time a public house called The Millstones, can clearly be seen on the superb photograph taken in 1870. Indeed, a man can be seen thatching the roof, so the owners could not have expected demolition in the immediate future! The cottages also appear on Medland and Taylor's drawing of the enlarged church. They were probably pulled down in the mid-seventies.

St. Lawrence's in 1870.

Middleton believed that these cottages, known as "The Old Thatch",[1] were possibly as ancient as the chapel itself, and this may well be correct. "With their thatched roofs and white-washed walls they formed picturesque ornaments of the neighbourhood. A writer to an early local newspaper,

[1] Middleton: page 117.

110

describing the cottages in his days says: 'In one of the cottages the inmates, when seated by their fireside, must have been within three feet of the rotting bodies of their neighbours in the graveyard.' "[1]

"The Old Thatch".

The Murphy Riots

In 1868 there were only about twenty Roman Catholics living in Denton and Hooley Hill. They walked to Ashton to hear Mass at St. Anne's, their parish church. In Ashton itself was a small community of Irish Catholics, living in a poor part of the town which was called "Little Ireland". Bishop Vaughan said at the time that not one Catholic family in Manchester or Salford could afford a carriage.[2] It was a largely immigrant community, treated with deep suspicion by the surrounding English.

This suspicion was intensified by reports in the newspapers of crimes committed by the Fenians – a league, based in the United States, for promoting revolution and the overthrow of English Government in Ireland. Also, it was feared by Protestants that Gladstone's Bill to disestablish the Church of Ireland was playing into the hands of Roman Catholics. There was a great deal of public anxiety and it was vital that rumour and mis-understanding should not multiply.

Realising how delicate the situation was, Father William Crombleholme, parish priest of St. Anne's, Ashton, called a meeting for his flock in the

[1] Middleton: page 57.
[2] Centenary Booklet of Denton St. Mary's Church and School, page 9.

Catholic school on Tuesday, January, 7th 1868. Its purpose was to condemn Fenianism. "There is no doubt," Father Crumbleholme insisted, "that the Irish people are quite equal to the English for their peaceableness, their honesty, their attention to their duties and for their social virtues." Irish people had as little to do with the outrages committed by Fenians as English people. Of course, Ireland laboured under grievances and Irishmen wanted self-government, but good Catholics strongly wished to disassociate themselves from scts of violence. The parish priest was supported in this by statements from the body of the meeting.[1]

Three days later, on Friday, January 10th, the National Protestant Institute held a large meeting in Ashton Town Hall. (The Reverend T. N. Farthing was on the platform). Intense indignation was expressed at Gladstone's proposal to disestablish the Church of Ireland. Priestcraft and Popery were condemned. "It is said that it is right to disestablish The Irish Church because Catholics are in the majority, but it is by majorities that the Devil rules the world!" – A remark greeted by laughter and cheers.

Ten days later, Mr. William Murphy, a forty-five year old Yorkshireman, arrived in Ashton from Stalybridge. He had come to exploit this unstable situation by delivering a series of lectures entitled "Popery and Puseyism." He had been stumping the country for some time and his lectures in Stalybridge (to audiences of eight hundred in the Foresters' Hall) had resulted in disturbances in the streets.

In Ashton he acquired Wright's Old Mill on Oldham Road and began a fortnight's lectures on the evening of Monday, January 20th. He was a skillful and practiced rabble-rouser of the worst kind, attracting audiences of working-class roughs who cheered, shouted, laughed and cracked jokes during the address. Mr. Murphy was accompanied each night by a bodyguard of seventy to eighty supporters from Stalybridge, armed with cudgels and shillelaghs. On entering the hall he would mount the platform, slowly look all around and ask, "Where are the Fenians?" He would then produce a revolver and lay it on the table in front of him, boasting that he needed no protection from the police!

The jist of his lectures can easily be summarised:

(1) The Pope is Antichrist and the Church of Rome is an empire of tyranny and error.

(2) Ireland – and all other Catholic countries – is enslaved.

(3) Priests are aiders and abetters of Fenians. Catholics owe allegience to a foreign Prince, (The Pope) and cannot be regarded as loyal British citizens.

---

[1] *Ashton Reporter*, 11th January, 1868.

(4) The country is going to the dogs because the Church of England is going neck and crop to Rome. (By "Puseyism" he means High Church practices within the Church of England and he points out that Gladstone is High Church.)

(5) Loyal Englishmen should become Orangemen, ready to defend truth and liberty. (Incidentally, there was a lodge of Orangemen in Denton at the time, meeting in the Coach and Horses on Hyde Road.)

The entrance fee to a lecture was one penny.

During the first lecture, windows were broken at the far end of the room. "I am sure," Murphy exclaimed, "if the Fenians come here they will get a warm reception." When silence had been restored, Mr. Flynn, (Murphy's right-hand man) said: "Now who are the breakers of the peace; is it Murphy who breaks the peace now? The fiends outside could not bear to hear of the exposure of their abominable doctrines and those stones which have broken the windows must have been thrown by some Popish dog." A few exasperated Catholics had allowed themselves to be goaded into retaliation. It was their first mistake.

On Tuesday (21st), one thousand five hundred people crowded into the mill. A Catholic in the audience was brave enough to try to argue with Mr. Murphy and was easily outwitted. Outside the hall a number of Irish women shouted insults and vindictive remarks and a large number of Special Constables were on duty. About ten o'clock a tremendous cheer went up inside the hall. The bodyguard formed up on either side of the entrance, Murphy appeared and fired a shot from his pistol into the air. He then marched at the head of a procession back to his lodgings and on the way an old woman threw a handful of mud at Mr. Flynn, a dangerous and foolish thing to do. However, a journalist from the *Ashton Reporter* who walked round the Irish quarter found all quiet. The great majority of Catholics were keeping to their homes.

On Wednesday, Murphy was shouted at in the streets as he and his bodyguard were on their way to the mill, but it was on the Thursday that things exploded. The room was crowded to the doors a full hour before the lecture was due to start. There was great excitement and when he arrived Murphy announced that he had had notice to quit his lodgings because the Papists had smashed his windows. He then denounced the Chief Constable as a truckler to Popery.

His address was entitled "The Seven Pretended Sacraments of Romanists" and in the middle of it there was another crash of breaking glass. Irish navvies had thrown stones and a young woman was badly cut about the head, blood running freely down her face. At once, the shout went up "To The Chapel; to Flag Alley" and lads began leaving the hall. Outside they were joined by many more who had been unable to get into the lectures. Singing "Rule Britannia" a very large crowd moved down Old Street to the Catholic Chapel in Burlington Street. A Policeman attempted to take a bludgeon away from a youth, but it fell to the ground and another seized it. The mob broke the large east window and some others. Then the cry was raised "To Charlestown Chapel". The procession re-formed and set off with Mr. Murphy and Mr. Flynn at the head. They had not gone far, however, when a large body of Police appeared. The journalist from the *Ashton Reporter* tells us that "as soon as Mr. Flynn saw the officers he left the position he had been occupying and stepped outside the ranks. Letting his hands fall by his side he assumed an innocent look and appeared as harmless as a lamb. The effect was ludicrous in the extreme."[1]

The Chief Constable induced Mr. Murphy and Mr. Flynn to return to their lodgings, the Concert Tavern which was about one hundred yards away. The mob hung around and at length Mr. Flynn came to the door and made a speech. He said that he and Mr. Murphy would like the people to go home, but they could please themselves. They did not go home. "On to Little Ireland" was the cry. The procession re-formed in the presence of the police and moved off to "Rule Britannia". When they got to Charles Street, youths rushed up it smashing windows with their sticks. The police managed to scare them off, but within a few minutes a gang of angry Irishmen came on the scene armed with pokers, brush handles, shillalahs and bludgeons. They could not – and would not – be restrained. They had acted on police advice in staying away from Murphy and now they had been attacked in their own homes. Shouting "send Murphy out of town" they headed for the presbytery, where Father Crombleholme and the Sisters of Mercy lived. They jammed the street in a state of great anxiety and were only calmed at length by the Mayor (T. H. Darnton, Esq.) who mounted the shoulders of a police officer to address them. He succeeded in getting them to return to their homes.

On the following night, Friday, the entrance fee was raised to sixpence to keep out the rough element and Mr. Murphy lectured on "The Confessional Unmasked". Large numbers of lads hung about the streets and some of them went down to St. Anne's Catholic Chapel in Burlington Street, only to find it guarded by 300 Irishmen armed with pokers, sticks, swords, knives and pistols. Luckily, the police managed to keep everything under control. By one o'clock in the morning they had persuaded the men to

[1] *Ashton Reporter*, 25th January, 1868.

disperse and taken from them enough weapons to fill "a West Indian Chief's armoury."[1]

On Sunday, Mr. Murphy conducted two church services in the mill and on the Monday he returned to the subject of "The Seven Pretended Sacraments of the Romanists," hoping, this time, to finish it! The audience was disorderly, making a rush for seats, many young women sitting on boys' knees! Mr. Murphy objected to newspapers calling the disturbances "Murphy Riots". They should be called "Priests' Riots" and Mr. Flynn added that they "had made Father Crombleholme dance"!

Murphy began his lecture by shouting at the top of his voice that when they were quiet he would bring their attention to "a fact in reference to the stained glass window in the babyhouse yonder." It was not stained glass. It was as common as a mill window – with painted paper stuck on! He then launched himself into a virulent tirade against Father Crombleholme, insisting that Italians hated Popery because the Pope stank under their noses.[2] But Murphy was, by now, past the peak of his popularity in Ashton. As the second week's lectures proceeded, interest tailed off and in February he returned to do more barn-storming in Stalybridge.

As for Father Crombleholme, a man of deep faith and great courage, he had no intention of retreating. He was planning to open a chapel of ease in Denton and within eighteen months, as we shall see, his endeavours were crowned with success.

The Rector's Health

Early in 1869 Walter Nicol left the parish. He had worked too hard, not only taking all services and carrying out all parochial duties without the help of a curate, but also trying to cope with the growing demands of Haughton Green. Furthermore, his wife was an invalid and his boys were growing up. At the beginning of March he went to the tiny hamlet of Newton St. Petrock near Holsworthy in Devon, where he was immediately installed as Rector.[3]

He was not allowed to leave Denton, however, without receiving tangible proof of his parishioners affection. On Friday, February 26th, he was presented with a purse containing fifty-five gold sovereigns and on the following Tuesday the teachers and scholars of St. Lawrence's Sunday School gave him "a beautiful timepiece" which was on view in the school-room the following evening. Mr. James Hartley, superintendent, hoped

[1] *Ashton Reporter*, February 1st, 1868.
[2] *Ashton Reporter*, February 1st, 1868.
[3] *Ashton Reporter*, February 27th, 1869.

that Mr. Nicol "might be successful in his future sphere of labour and regain his health."[1]

But it was too late. He is able to carry out his duties for only eighteen months before some illness gets the better of him. On May 25th, 1872 he died and was buried five days later at the west end of the church near the south-west corner of the tower. He was sixty-seven.[2]

[1] *North Cheshire Herald*, March 6th, 1869.
[2] Letter from the Reverend George E. Chippington, M.A., the present Incumbent.

CHAPTER FIVE

THE OLD CHURCH IS ENLARGED

IN VICTORIAN times, the laity of the Church of England believed that a clergyman should be a prosperous gentleman of the upper middle-class with a degree from either Oxford or Cambridge. Charles James Bowen met this ideal in full. He was a Cambridge man, an impressive orator and a High Tory!

The Rev. Charles James Bowen,
Rector 1869-1881.

On his first Sunday in the parish he surprised the crowded church by preaching in his white surplice. This had never been done before in St. Lawrence's. Although all clergy conducted the service in a surplice, they changed into a black gown to deliver the sermon. To preach in a surplice was regarded as high church. Mr. Bowen was careful to explain his action and gave three reasons for it: First, he had been in the habit of doing so; second, he had no black gown and third, the use of the surplice had been sanctioned by the Privy Council. He mentioned this for the satisfaction of those who might suspect him of a tendency to Romanism or Ritualism, in which respect he trusted they would find but little difference between himself and their late pastor. He then preached from Judges, Chapter 3, verse 20: "I have a message from God unto thee." The sermon was masterly and the people realised that their new rector was a fine preacher.[1]

[1] *Ashton Reporter*, March 6th, 1869.

Mr. Bowen had no intention of trying to do all the work of the parish himself. Within three months he was joined by his first curate, The Revd. J. F. Brien and in the next five years had no less than six! They followed each other in quick succession, sometimes staying only one year and we cannot help suspecting that they were unhappy and glad to leave. Was their Rector too authoritative and autocratic? It is probable, from what we know of him that he was.[1]

Little Old St. Mary's

On the 29th May, 1869, the foundation stone of a Roman Catholic school-cum-chapel was laid on a piece of ground which we know today as the corner of Duke Street and Market Street. Father Combleholme's dream had come true. Mr. Bowen and the people of St. Lawrence's would be annoyed to see a new place of worship, but would dismiss it from their minds contemptuously as an event not worthy of notice.

For the next twenty years St. Mary's depended on the priests of St. Anne's, Ashton. They came on horse-back to say Mass and administer the Sacraments to the tiny congregation of Denton Catholics. Life was hard for them. Many Denton people would have heard Murphy in Ashton and in June 1868 he had held a series of his lectures in Hyde. Windows in little St. Mary's were so frequently broken that they had to be protected by metal grilles. The congregation numbered about twenty to thirty, increased by Irish labourers to about sixty at harvest times.[2]

In the early days the day school consisted simply of one small class of children, but there was also a class for adults at night. This was first examined by the headmistress of St. Anne's, Ashton in 1870 and was, of course, a night school to teach men and women to read and write. The school fees were fourpence a week.[3] From such humble beginnings grew the church which today has far larger congregations than any other church in Denton.

Riding the Stang

During the Wakes of 1872 Samuel Hadfield saw a strange incident which he related to Middleton many year later. A man named Hickling who had been accused of poisoning his wife was acquitted at Chester

[1] The Curates were:— J. F. Brien, May 1869–Nov. 1870; J. H. Hickey, May, 1870–April, 1871; A. S. L. Sparling, April, 1871–April, 1872; Evan Harris, February, 1872–February, 1873; J. Turner, May, 1872–August, 1872; Charles Morris, April, 1873–March, 1875.

 St. Mary's Souvenir Brochure (1963).

[3] Centenary Booklet, page 9. "Little Old St. Mary's" as it became known, was demolished in 1961 to make way for the present church.

Assizes. It was known, however, that he was associating with a young widow who lived in Bentley's Buildings, Broom Lane. When the news of the acquittal became known, Hadfield's neighbours were on the look-out for Hickling, feeling certain that he would visit the lady. He did – on the Thursday of Denton Wakes. A crowd at once gathered in front of the door and began to groan and hiss. Before long, a reporter from the *North Cheshire Herald*[1] was on the scene to record it in detail:—

> "Finding, however, that they might as well attempt to draw a badger as to get him to leave the house, a clothes prop was soon improvised into a gibbet, on which to hang an effigy of Hickling, which was quickly made of straw, stuffed into a pair of white pants; on the top of them was an old black coat, similarly stuffed, great pains having been taken with the arms. Crowning the whole was a cap, displaying a mask with a black nose; in the right hand was placed a mousetrap and in the left a weathercock. Thus arrayed, it was borne aloft in a procession past the house, headed by a tin-pot band, composed of tin whistles, bells, trays and anything and everything which would make a noise."

This crude and heartless exhibition was known as "Riding the Stang" – an attempt on the part of the community to ensure observance of the laws governing matrimony. Very probably this was the last example of it in the life of Denton and the *North Cheshire Herald* saw it out to the end:—

> "About half-past two the procession moved away with the intention of making a circuitous route to Hickling's residence at Flowery Field, there to burn the effigy. The appearance of the processionists was ludicrous in the extreme. An old woman, dressed most fantastically, with a fancy oilcloth for a shawl and a muslim window blind for a veil, personated the widow, whilst many hatters were also dressed up for the occasion, but the characters they personated were only suggestive of the gallows and its attendants; for a more gallows-looking lot never took part in a procession.

> "Seeing the turn events had taken, it was very evident that the police hardly knew what course to take in reference to the matter. However, after following the procession along Hyde Road and Stockport Road, and when near to the Chapel Green, the police intimated to the party who was carrying the effigy that if it was not taken out of the streets it would be taken from them. This warning took effect and in Mr. Knowles' field it was pulled to pieces. But some of the

---

[1] *North Cheshire Herald*, August 17th, 1872. Quoted by Middleton: page 131. Could Samuel Hadfield himself have been the reporter? He lived in Broom Lane.

women, proverbially characteristic of their sex, went to the shavings and set them on fire and the police became possessed of the coat and trousers. Thus ended the hanging and effigy-burning. But so late as ten o'clock groups of people were congregated in the neighbourhood of Bentley's Buildings and the event has been the subject of endless gossip ever since."[1]

Considerable Enlargement

One of the first and most important decisions Mr. Bowen made was to enlarge the old church. It was far too small for the growing parish and something had to be done. Moreover, The Wesleyans had decided to build themselves a new church, school and manse on Hyde Road and the foundation stone was laid on August 7th, 1871. Such a challenge could not be ignored, for Mr. Bowen would certainly feel irritated by Methodists with their strong social conscience, Liberal politics and smug teetotalism![2]

July 28th, 1872 was Sermons Sunday. The church was found to be far too small and on the following Wednesday the work of enlarging it began. It took eight months and services were held in St. Lawrence's school until the following April. Sunday the sixth was a great day and it was described at length in *The Ashton Reporter*.

"This Church was re-opened on Sunday last, after undergoing considerable enlargement, the present building being more than double the size of the old one. The old part of the church has, however, hardly been touched at all; but the new work has been carried out in such a manner as to retain the quaint peculiar character of the ancient building. The old church was of the simplest form, consisting of a parallelogram about 26 yards long by rather more than 8 yards wide. It seems originally to have had no chancel, but during the incumbency of Mr. Greswell (a former rector) a chancel – or at least a tiny eastern recess – little more than 8 feet by 6 feet was built. There is now a spacious chancel, with arcaded open screens dividing it from the nave and the side aisles. Some old carved oak panels, which were probably part of the former seating, have been inserted in the choir seats. The sanctuary – or easternmost part of the chancel – has wooden traceried arcading round the lower part, and above this a wooden diaper, with stamped plaster. The Sedilia and credence are of pitch pine, as are (with a few exceptions) the rest of the fittings. The east

[1] Another account of "Riding the Stang" can be found in Appendix VIII of The Village of Ecclesfield by David Hey, M. A. (1968, *The Advertiser Press Ltd.*, Huddersfield).
[2] Nearly all Non-conformists had become Abstainers by 1870.

window contains stained glass (by Messrs. Lavers, Banard and West-lake) with a representation of the crucifixion in the centre light, the four acts of Mercy being arranged in the lights on either side. The additional accommodation is contained in short north and south aisles, half of each of which flank the nave, and the other half the chancel. In forming the opening between the new aisles and the nave, the ancient construction has not been interfered with; but the lath and plaster work between the oak supports has merely been removed. The old mode of construction – that is, the timber framing, filled in between with lath and plaster, outside and in – has been maintained throughout; and whatever may be its merits or demerits, it is incontesible that it is a most picturesque mode of building. The roof is covered with grey-stone slates, with plain stone ridge, with the exception of that on the chancel, which is slightly ornamental. There are boldly projecting eaves and gables, and low broad mullioned windows. The eastern cross is worked in the shape of the symbol of St. Lawrence, to whom the church is dedicated. There is further work already in the hands of the architects – Messrs. Medland and Henry Taylor. For instance, the improvement of the west gallery, the formation of a new baptistery at the north-west corner of the church, and a new turret, and a lean-to porch to the west door. It is also greatly desired to complete the restoration of the interior, the clearing of the whitewash off the roof and wall timbers and to remove what now conceals what is characteristic and beautiful in the old church.

"The morning preacher was the Lord Bishop of Manchester; the preacher in the afternoon, the Rev. C. Morris; and in the evening the Rev. E. D. Jackson, Rector of Heaton Chapel. The congregations were very large, especially in the morning when the Lord Bishop preached. His Lordship, as is his custom, preached a most eloquent sermon, adapted judiciously to the place and the occasion, and containing much sound practical advice, and large and liberal views. The services of Miss Thorley of Manchester, were secured for the occasion and she sang "Pious Orgies" and the choir assisted by a full chorus, sang "O Father whose almight power," both from the oratorios of "Judas Maccabaeus" and Beethoven's "Hallelujah". The whole, singing as well as the preaching, was worthy of the sacred occasion, and, what was perhaps not the least to be despised, the collections, which were in aid of the funds for enlarging the church, realised the large figure of £109."[1]

[1] *Ashton Reporter*, 12th April, 1873.

Who was the bishop who preached in the morning expressing such "large and liberal views"? James Fraser (1818–1885) whose statue stands today in Albert Square. He was the second Bishop of Manchester and had been nominated by Gladstone. As bishop (1870–1885) he became immensely popular with the working-classes and it is Fraser's sermons that Samuel Hadfield collected so keenly.

As soon as he had been consecrated bishop, he started to conduct services in mills and factories during dinner hours and concerned himself with the problems of bargemen and dustmen. At the Leeds Church Congress in 1872 he created a sensation by defending the right of agricultiral labourers to form a trade union and he praised their leader – a Primitive Methodist called Joseph Arch.

One wonders what the "big men" at St. Lawrence's church thought to such a Bishop. John Bentley, Church Warden (1816–1893) of Haughton Hall, John Gould (1806–1879), Peter Rothwell (1821–1899), manager of Denton collieries, John Taylor, Church Warden, and many others would be there listening to what they would consider to be a disturbingly left-wing man. They probably sat in solemn silence, feeling somewhat suspicious and resentful, but one man in the congregation enjoyed the sermon very much indeed – Samuel Hadfield. He must have been delighted that his hero-bishop was preaching in *his* church and he noted the text: "Be still and know that I am God," (Psalm 46, verse 10).[1]

The following Sunday, (April 13th) special services continued. The Revd. W. Ogden of St. Peter's, Ashton, preached in the morning. The Revd. T. Wolesley Lewis of Cheltenham College preached in the afternoon and the Rector in the evening. Evening services were now held every Sunday in St. Lawrence's whilst the curates continued to take evening services in the Iron School at Haughton Green. Mr. Bowen took as his subject "Denton past and Denton present." The services were fully choral and in the afternoon Mr. Mark Stafford of Hyde sang "He was despised" and "Lift up your heads". The collections amounted to about £20.[2]

The Rector Writes a Hymn

The cost of the enlargement was over £1,700 and to help defray the expenses a broadsheet was printed containing the words and music of a new hymn written by Mr. Bowen. At the top was a picture of the church as it used to be when the great yew tree stood in the churchyard. The

[1] It was a rambling sermon, reported fully in the *North Cheshire Herald* (April 12th, 1873). It contained passages against rivalry between denominations and greed in business men.
[2] *Ashton Reporter*, 19th April, 1873.

drawing was by Richard Edwin Bibby, a Haughtonian and industrial chemist. At the bottom was the architects' drawing of the newly enlarged church and in between came these words:—

I love to see our antient church
Around whose sacred shade
The ashes of our fore-fathers
In trusting faith are laid.

I love to hear its chiming bell
When it invites to prayer;
I love to hear its people say
Come let us worship there.

I love our dear old English Church
And Apostolic Creed,
For it shows to me the Saviour
That I a sinner need.

I love her solemn Litany
Her lessons slowly read;
In solemn silence, too, I love
Her Burial of the Dead.

I love her Book of Common Prayer
So simple, so sublime;
The martyrs' prayers and prayers of saints
Throughout all Christian time.

I love them all, for all express
My heart's intense desire;
And, as I utter them I feel
The Spirit's kindling fire.

Oh, yes! I love our antient Church
And like my trusting sires
I too would rest beneath its shade
When this frail life expires.

Till every waiting saint that sleeps
A living stone shall rise,
To form an immaterial Church
More noble in the skies.

DENTON CHURCH A CENTURY AGO, FROM A DRAWING BY R. E. BIBBY.

WOODBINE

Words adapted by the
Rev⁴ C. J. Bowen M.A.

I love to see our an-tient Church A round whose sa-cred shade

The ash-es of our fore-fa-thers In trust-ing faith are laid

I love to hear its chiming bell,
  When it invites to prayer ;
I love to hear its people say,
  Come let us worship there.

I love our dear old English Church,
  And Apostolic Creed,
For it shows to me the Saviour,
  That I a sinner need.

I love her solemn Litany,
  Her lessons slowly read ;
In solemn silence, too, I love
  Her Burial of the Dead.

I love her Book of Common Prayer,
  So simple, so sublime ;
The martyrs' prayers and prayers of saints
  Throughout all Christian time.

I love them all, for all express
  My heart's intense desire ;
And, as I utter them, I feel
  The Spirit's kindling fire.

Oh, yes ! I love our antient Church ;
  And like my trusting sires,
I too would rest beneath its shade,
  When this frail life expires.

Till every waiting saint that sleeps,
  A living stone shall rise,
To form an immaterial Church,
  More noble in the skies.

Amen.

DENTON OLD CHURCH AS ENLARGED IN 1872.—MEDLAND & TAYLOR, ARCHITECTS.

Lithographed by W. TOLLEY, Manchester.

Woodbine

The tune, "Woodbine" had been written by Thomas Newton of Ashton-under-Lyne, and (the broadsheet states) the "words adapted by the Revd. C. J. Bowen, M.A." Adapted from what? Possibly from "We love the place, O God," which had been written in 1827, but the parallel is not close.

"I love to see our antient church" became St. Lawrence's own special hymn and when we look at it closely three things strike us; first, it doesn't mention the enlargement at all; secondly, it is intensely Church of England and thirdly, it is almost obsessed with death, ashes and graveyards. It didn't mention the enlargement because there would be strong feelings amongst some parishioners that Mr. Bowen was ruining the old church. The hymn is intended to help to assuage their feelings, by concentrating on the fact that it is very "antient". It has a great deal to say about the excellence of the Prayer Book in order to make it plain that Church of England services are superior to those of all other denominations – especially the free churches which had no Prayer Book at all! But Mr. Bowen, (like many Victorians) was so pre-occupied with death that he forgets to mention the most important service of all – The Holy Communion! As for caring for those worse off than ourselves and spreading the love of Christ – these things receive no mention! It was an inward-looking, self-centred hymn, shot through with Victorian religiosity – and an undoubted hit!

The Hangman Cheated
The church had only been enlarged six weeks when a dreadful event shook the town. Early on Monday, May 19th, James Etchells, a blacksmith of Dukinfield brutally murdered his wife by smashing her skull with a hammer whilst she lay in bed. Running out of the house he made for Denton. Passing the newly enlarged church, he turned down Town Lane and hanged himself in a copse in fields belonging to Hyde Hall farm. The body, found by a labourer, was taken to The Chapelhouse, where it lay for two days attracting a continuous stream of viewers. "Much regret was expressed that he had cheated the hangman of his job," for it was said that he had often treated his wife brutally.[1]

The Annual Tea Party
When Mr. Bowen came to St. Lawrence's he instituted an Annual Church Tea Party, which was held each October. The bishop returned as special guest to the 1873 Party and the speech he made must have been one of the most important and memorable that our parishioners had ever

[1] *Ashton Reporter*, 24th May, 1873.

heard from a bishop. Being a shrewd man and knowing something of Denton Old Church, he devoted his talk to two matters – rented pews and politics.

"A church with rented pews may be your idea of a church", he said, "but it is certainly not mine. I do not like those invidious distinctions which give the well-to-do people the best places in church. That was not the spirit of the Apostle of Our Lord Jesus Christ." He then quoted the Letter of James, Chapter 2: "If there come unto your assembly a man with a gold ring, in goodly apparel, and there come in also a poor man in vile raiment; and ye have respect to him that weareth the gay clothing and say unto him, Sit thou here in a good place; and say to the poor, Stand thou there, or sit here under my footstool: Are ye not then partial in yourselves and are become judges of evil thoughts?"[1] The bishop then said that on the previous day he had preached on that text to a wealthy congregation in Manchester.

The gathering at the Tea Party applauded the bishop at this point, but the Rector and the "big men" controlling St. Lawrence's had no intention of abolishing rented pews. At the Annual Vestry held the previous April only six men were present with the Rev. C. J. Bowen.[2] They controlled the church completely and their ears were closed to what the bishop was saying. Alas, pew rents were not finally abolished in St. Lawrence's until 1955!! May God forgive us![3]

The second part of the bishop's speech was even more important than the first. "I know," he said, "that it was sometimes thought that a Churchman must be a Conservative and that a Conservative must be a Churchman, but I take the liberty of saying that there are many good Churchmen who are sincere Liberals and many good Liberals who are Churchmen." This too was greeted with applause and he enlarged on it at some length. He hoped that in the House of God the bitterness of political controversy would be kept at bay.[4] It was a note which badly needed sounding, but those at whom it was chiefly directed chose to ignore it. Most members of the Established Church *were* Conservatives and most Non-conformists were not. They were scarcely on speaking terms and, as we shall now see, it often led to acrimonious exchanges.

[1] Letter of James, Chapter 2 verses 2–4 (Authorised Version).
[2] *Ashton Reporter*, 19th April, 1873.
[3] Canon J. J. Stevenson, who was Rector at the time writes in a letter to the Author: "Yes, it was in our time that pew rents were abolished. That was a struggle! One of our greatest satisfactions in St. Lawrence's was the day we went through the church and removed the small pieces of paper. I thought the Irish Church was conservative but was appalled that such things existed in an English Parish."
[4] *Ashton Reporter*, 29th October, 1873.

Christian Enemies

In March, 1872, Mr. E. Baker Jones who was schoolmaster of the Free Church Schools, had given a lecture to a crowded audience on The History of Denton. During the course of it, he made certain remarks upon two Denton clergymen and the journalist from the *Ashton Reporter* considered these remarks in very bad taste.[1]

Without doubt, Mr. Jones was referring to the Rectors of Christ Church and St. Lawrence's. He would comment on their political views and the fact that they jealously defended the privileged position of the Established Church. The lecture became a talking-point in Denton and produced an extremely forthright letter from an anonymous correspondent to the *Ashton Reporter.*

"Sir, – A good deal of noise has been made by a few fussy folk in condemnation of Mr. Jones's lecture on Denton. His plain speaking on one point has offended mother church. Now it strikes me that these poor scribblers should be economical and save their ink. They are on the wrong end of the plank. Oh how they love our parsons! So do not I! I will lay a few questions before the village; answers to them will much oblige a large number of your subscribers. The answers can be sent to the post office for my care. They are these; who was it said (a good many years ago) that twelve shillings a week was sufficient for working men? Who was it that had to make a public apology for slandering a gentleman now dead? Who was it said of Dissent that it was irreligious? Who was it condemned the Act of Parliament which gave the right to Nonconformists to marry in their own chapels? Who is it that has never been the workman's true friend? One answer will do for all these questions.[2] Ah, surely we have dropped on bad times; but things will change shortly, we hope, for the better.[3] Mr. Jones was not half heavy enough and I would advise him to repeat his lecture "with additions" and shall be glad to supply him with a whole "budget" of reliable information. His calumniators are only poor churchlings who dare not refuse to yelp when their master bids. – I am, yours respectfully – An OBSERVER

DENTON, APRIL 2nd, 1872."

Many more years were to go by before the divided Christian Church could even begin to heal wounds such as these.

[1] *Ashton Reporter*, 23rd March, 1872.
[2] The answer is obvious – The Rev. T. N. Farthing, Rector of Christ Church.
[3] He was about to leave Christ Church.

The Absurd Boundary

With Mr. Bowen's zealous work on behalf of St. Lawrence's we must contrast the role he played in local government, but before allowing the astonishing story to unfold, let us remind ourselves once more that Denton and Haughton were two separate townships divided by a completely artificial boundary. Denton consisted of all the land on the left-hand side of Stockport Road as one travels from Three Lane Ends through Crown Point and along Ashton Road to the boundary with Audenshaw, but in addition there was a large piece of land to the RIGHT-hand side of Stockport Road and Ashton Road as a glance at the map on page 129 will show. Haughton had no centre at all, but straggled as it followed the river from Audenshaw right round to Haughton Dale. There was no logic or common sense in such a boundary, but the two townships were determined to remain separate and did so until 1894.

Mr. Bowen's rectory stood in Haughton, on Vaudry Lane. He did not, therefore, have to pay rates to the Denton Local Board of Health which had been set up in 1857. Dentonians were proud of the fact that their town had been one of the first in the country to adopt the Public Health Act and set up a Local Board with five committees: (1) Highway and Street Improvement; (2) Nuisance Committee; (3) Lighting, Building and Market Committee; Finance Committee; (5) General Purposes Committee. At their monthly meetings, elected members of the Board tried to grapple with all those problems which a growing industrial town had to face – especially questions affecting sanitary conditions. They needed money and money came from the rates, but Haughton had no Local Board, so whilst Denton sought to improve itself, Haughton did next to nothing.

The Nuisance Committee

How was the Denton Local Board getting along in the early seventies? Badly. The members of the Nuisance Committee had become apathetic and there were many complaints about the filthy state of the streets and cesspools.[1] Things sank to such a low ebb that an anonymous journalist who wrote a column in the *Ashton Reporter* (which he called "Casual Jottings") began to pillory the Board. He was, as we shall see, a very enlightened man to whom the general public were indebted, but never was a column in a newspaper more foolishly named! They were not "jottings"; they were sustained attacks upon social abuses. And they were anything but "casual"! Take this, for example on May 18th, 1872.

[1] *Ashton Reporter*, February 11th, 1871.

128

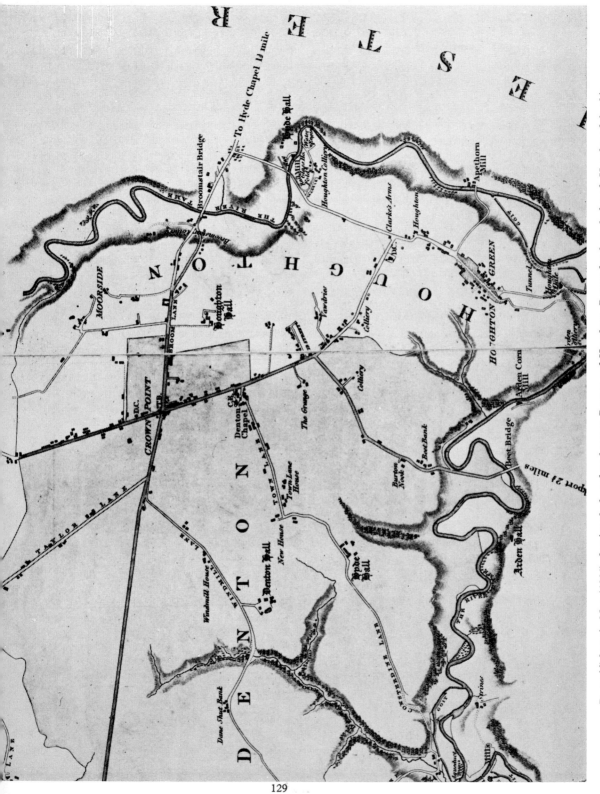

Part of Johnson's Map (1820) showing the boundary between Denton and Haughton. Denton has been darkened, Haughton left white.

"Happy is the man who possesses an easy, cool temperament that guides him through the world without ever being ruffled or in any way put about. No doubt there are such men if we knew where to find them and, if we mistake not, they are to be found in Denton and they form the Nuisance Committee of the Denton Local Board. The gentlemen who compose this committee take matters coolly enough. There is no flurry – no hurry – with them. The duties of their office don't disturb them in the least. Stinks and stenches may abound, stagnant abominations and pregnant pollutions may exist, but what is that to them? Nuisances may be reported week after week and month after month, but still, what is that to them? They take matters so easily that they find it too much trouble to meet once a month. On Monday week, they should have met half an hour before the Board Meeting and the Inspector was present to give in his report, but no Committee appeared. Now, everyone will say that the duties devolving upon a Nuisance Committee are the most important of all that attach to a Board of Health, for, if words have any meaning, it is the primary duty of a Board of Health to look after the health of the people living in the district for which it has been formed. In Denton, however, the health of the inhabitants seems to be the last consideration. Nuisances have been reported months ago, but they are allowed to exist still. This state of things, to say the least of it, is not as it should be."

The summer of 1872 was very wet and there were five cases of smallpox in June.[1] The Nuisance Committee could not find anywhere to tip night-soil so many ashpits remained unemptied until December, when they appointed a certain Swindells as the nightsoil man, but he was so un-satisfactory that they sacked him in January. Nevertheless, progress was being made and the *Ashton Reporter* was able to give the world this news on January, 18th, 1873:—

"The Nuisance Committee of the Denton Local Board are at last bestirring themselves in earnest and adopting measures for the effectual removal and suppression of nuisances. They have got a horse and cart of their own and engaged a few scavengers; and they are prepared to make contracts with the surrounding farmers for the nightsoil. The Committee have also resolved to make the butchers in the township provide tubs, or suitable receptacles for their offal and refuse and these must be emptied twice a week in the summer season and once a

[1] *Ashton Reporter*, June 22nd, 1872.

130

week in winter. "It is never too late to mend" and actuated by this sentiment, the Committee are mending their ways at last and taking the necessary steps to put the township in a proper sanitary condition. They are taking time by the forelock, knowing that the Public Health Act[1] will soon compel them to use such measures as they are now adopting in the interests of the public health."

By July, all butchers except Mr. John Redfern had been provided with receptacles[2] and things had improved generally, but Mr. Howard Ashton still had an open cesspool which was soaking through the closet of his premises on Ashton Road. Mr. George Elliot was engaged to remove nightsoil and take charge of the horse and cart at a weekly wage of twenty-two shillings.[3]

The new Health Act required each Local Board to appoint a medical officer. The journalist writing "Casual Jottings" applauded the fact, but could not prevent himself from saying what he thought about it when Dr. W. J. Allkin was given the position. "He is related to one of the largest property owners in the district and he will not be able to carry out his duties under the Act impartially. Portions of that property are the worst in the township in a sanitary point, and such as no other Board but an easy-going one like Denton would have tolerated so long."[4]

In March he reported in "Casual Jottings" that the Medical Officer had done nothing and attended no meetings, yet there was so much fever in the town that there had been a funeral a day for the last 14 days.[5] It was not until May that Dr. Allkin submitted his first report and (says "Casual Jottings") "a more meagre and unsatisfactory document could not well be conceived."[6]

Nevertheless, the Denton Local Board was slowly pressing ahead, putting a system of sewers under the roads, cobbling streets and flagging pavements. They borrowed a further £600 to help pay for the sewers in October, 1874 and at their annual dinner held in the King's Head in February, 1875, great satisfaction was expressed at the progress being made. Mr. Brooks, clerk to the Board, said that in London a short time after the sewering and paving of the streets, the death-rate diminished by sixty per cent.[7] This was the reason for Denton's policy.

[1] A new Public Health Act had been passed in August, 1872.
[2] 12th July, 1973.
[3] *Ashton Reporter*, 9th August, 1873.
[4] *Ashton Reporter*, 3rd January, 1874.
[5] 21st March, 1874.
[6] 23rd May, 1874.
[7] *Ashton Reporter*, 13th February, 1875.

Lord Denton and Lady Haughton

But Denton's policy was not Haughton's. In exasperation "Casual Jottings" bursts out – "The township spends not a farthing on sanitary improvements. Haughton has no system of sewerage. Not a penny has been spent. There is not even a rate laid!"[1]

As we have seen, Denton was not a very sweet-smelling place. Haughton was far worse. It must have stank to high heaven in hot weather, but the rate-payers of the township were in no hurry to rectify matters. They were living in a very cheap locality and the last thing they wanted was to be amalgamated with Denton and be compelled to pay their rates.

In October 1872, the Denton Local Board had had the impertinence to suggest that the townships be united and had actually sent a letter to London suggesting this. Reaction was immediate. Rate-payers of Haughton held a well-attended meeting in St. Lawrence's School with The Revd. C. J. Bowen in the chair. They refused to unite with Denton. Denton is in debt. They want our money. So they called for the formation of a separate Haughton Local Board and Mr. Bowen gave them his full support. He pointed out, however, that the town had not been completely without a sanitary Authority of any kind. There had been a Haughton Sewer Authority of which he had been chairman, but it was now defunct through lack of funds. Nevertheless, he "put great stress on the fact that the Haughton Sewers Authority had spent less than a £10 note and that the greater portion of that went on rent, salary of the clerk and advertising." Alas, Mr. Bowen did not know that the journalist in charge of "Casual Jottings" was in the audience. This amazing confession stunned him. "Well might the Chairman ask," he writes, "where could they find a township with a population of 4,276 whose local affairs had been conducted more economically!"[2]

The situation was as clear as a summer's day. The Revd. C. J. Bowen, who lived in a large rectory, had sided with the leading rate-payers of Haughton – some of whom were "big men" at St. Lawrence's – in order to avoid paying rates for something as useless and unnecessary as a system of underground sewers. His short-sighted attitude is pitiful. Instead of offering enlightened leadership in order to improve public health, he was behaving like the worst kind of Victorian Tory. It comes as no surprise, then, to find "Casual Jottings" launching into this magnificent broadside:—

"The Rev. Charles James Bowen is no ordinary personage, for such is the range and versatility of his genius that he is equally "at home"

[1] *Ashton Reporter*, 26th April, 1873.
[2] *Ashton Reporter*, 26th October, 1872.

whether expounding Divine Law from the pulpit at Denton Old Church, or explaining human law from a temporary rostrum in the Denton and Haughton National School, or hunting out the stinks that so frequently impinge upon and so disagreeably titillate the olfactory nerves of the good people of Haughton. The Haughtonians too, as they ought to do, rightly appreciate the wonderful gifts of this "Admirable Crichton" of modern times; but his parishioners of Denton – and by the by his church is situated in that township – are somewhat sceptical about these transcendant abilities of his and there are not a few of them who hesitate not to say that it would beseem him better to mind his preaching more and his speechifying less and it would be more in consonance with his profession, if, instead of visiting these stench-pots and cesspools as he boasts he has done, he would visit more frequently "the haunts and homes" of the sick, the afflicted and the dying and offer them words of spiritual comfort and consolation; but those who make such assertions must belong to that large class of people who mind everybody else's business but their own and who, moreover, forget that "cleanliness is next to godliness", and that if a parson can make his parishioners cleanly he can soon make them godly. One of the Rev. Charles James Bowen's great gifts is his powers of oratory and it can be be truly said of him in the words of the Latin poet – PROFESSUS GRANDIA TURGET: NEC FACUNDIA DESERET HUNC; NEC LUCIDUS ORDO,"[1]

In April 1873, a Government Inspector, Mr. Arnold Taylor, was sent to look at Haughton. He reported that there was no system of drainage in Haughton and recommended that it be annexed to Denton Local Board. He could not see the point of an artificial boundary dividing what was obviously *one* industrial town.

The Haughtonians were infuriated by this common-sense approach and held another meeting in St. Lawrence's School at which they appointed a three-man deputation which would go to London and wait upon the Secretary of State. The three were The Revd. C. J. Bowen, Mr. John Taylor (one of St. Lawrence's Church Wardens) and Mr. William Walton, (son of Mr. James Walton, the owner of Haughton Dale Mills)[2] – all strong Conservatives with an absolute horror of "squandering public money!"

The deputation neither succeeded nor failed. Things remained at a standstill for four years, during which Denton continued to develop whilst

[1] *Ashton Reporter*, 25th January, 1873. The Latin means, "Having made splendid utterance he is turgid; eloquence will not fail him, nor clarity of judgement." It's a rough quotation from Horace.
[2] *Ashton Reporter*, 3rd May, 1873.

Haughton remained as it was. The absurdity of it came out clearly in August, 1875, when Denton announced more plans for improvement and "Casual Jottings" once more took up the cudgels.

> "The Deputy Clerk informed the Board that in respect to the flagging of the footpaths, a Government official would come down soon. Would it not be well to sound the Government official when he comes down about the increased and increasing desirableness of having Haughton annexed to Denton? The necessity of this union might be forcibly pointed out in connection with Ashton Road. While the footpaths of the other roads are to be flagged, Ashton Road, which requires it above all others, will be left as it is. Denton has no power to flag it and Haughton will not. Indeed Haughton will do nothing. It has been already twice declared by Mr. Arnold Taylor, Government inspector, as an unsewered place and it is still as it was then and likely to remain so, until some strong Authority takes it in hand. One would expect that the Revd. Charles James Bowen would employ his oratory on behalf of poor neglected Haughton. But perhaps he is carrying out the adage – that "he who goes to Rome must do as they do in Rome" – by contenting himself with walking in the groove made by the older guardians and doing as they do."[1]

At the end of August Mr. Bowen was given permission to set a parochial committee to deal with Haughton under the Rural Sanitary Authority. This was a small step towards his much hoped-for Haughton Local Board, but the committee was virtually powerless. "Casual Jottings" commented: "People will wait with some curiosity to see what great things this new authority with the Rev. Charles James Bowen at its head will do. Will its action be a duplicate of the celebrated £10 note policy? Time will tell."[2]

Time did tell. In 1877 Whitehall gave in and allowed the formation of a separate Haughton Local Board. Elections were held and the first meeting took place in the room over the Overseer's office, Haughton, on June 20th. At it, the Rev. C. J. Bowen was unanimously elected chairman. The ratepayers of Haughton were pleased, for although they must now equip the town with a system of underground sewers, they could be certain that it would be done with that stringent economy for which the Rector was justly famous.!

[1] *Ashton Reporter*, 7th August, 1875.
[2] *Ashton Reporter*, 28th August, 1875.

St. Mary's Haughton Dale

James Walton (1802–1883) was the largest employer in Haughton Green and the perfect example of what a successful Victorian industrialist should be. From an early age he had shown something of a genius for invention and his improvements to cotton-spinning machinery together with his business acumen made him extremely wealthy. At his death several newspapers, including *The Times*, carried his obituary.[1]

The card-making and wire-drawing mill which he had established in Haughton Dale in 1853 was built on to an older mill – Haughton Dale Cotton mill – which he had bought. It was leased out by him to Messrs. Wood and Co. but had to close down in May, 1873.[2] Fortunately, the two hundred people made redundant soon found other jobs and although hatting was suffering from a depression,[3] the people of Haughton Green did not fear hard times, but looked to Mr. Walton with affection and respect, knowing that he had their well-being at heart. In 1868, he had purchased a large house and estate at Dolforgan in Wales to which he retired, leaving his son William, who lived in Harrytown Hall, to look after Haughton Dale Mills.

It was clear to everyone that Haughton Green needed a church of its own and in the early seventies the Walton family decided that the time had come to act. Apart from a Church Building Society grant, the cost was borne entirely by them. Medland and Taylor, the architects who had enlarged St. Lawrence's, were engaged to design something suitable and, as we can see for ourselves, it is an excellent example of their asymmetrical style. Nikolaus Pevsner, who is one of Britain's foremost authorities on architecture, calls them arch-rogues because of the way in which they mixed up traditional styles of architecture into a hotch-potch. "Their inventiveness of perversities and their crotchety motifs are unlimited", says Pevsner, "yet they were never short of clients."[4] He calls St. Mary's Haughton Green and St. Anne's, Haughton (1882) two of the most wilful of their designs, but he speaks as a purist who regards architecture as a high form of art. To us both churches are gems of the Victorian era, accurately reflecting popular taste.

The Grand Procession

By 1874 all was ready for the laying of the foundation stone which took place on Saturday, April 11th. A procession, nearly a mile long, set off

[1] See Appendix V for a summary of his life.
[2] *Ashton Reporter*, May 10th, 1873.
[3] *Ashton Reporter*, December 27th, 1873.
[4] N. Pevsner: The Buildings of England: South Lancashire (Penguin 1969), page 43.

from Denton's market square at 3 p.m. Almost everyone turned out to see it as it moved along Stockport Road up to the Clarke's Arms, swinging right to go down to the site of the church. First came the band leading the scholars of Haughton Dale Sunday School, marching six abreast. Then came St. Lawrence's Sunday School, followed by Christ Church Sunday School, each led by their teachers and clergy. Following them came the strange sight of the Fire Brigade with their engine! Samuel Hadfield would be pleased to see it because Denton's Volunteer Fire Brigade had been set up at his suggestion nine years earlier.[1] This was followed by the United Order of Oddfellows carrying a beautiful banner and marching behind it four abreast. The Loyal Orange Lodges also marched four abreast and drew from the crowd admiring comments – three were dressed in their gowns, there were sword bearers and four little boys carried an open Bible. Lastly, came the Free Masons.

On arriving at the site of the church, the children divided, three on either side and formed a circle round the foundation stone. The fire engine, with the Brigade on either side, remained at the entrance to the ground. The Orders then filed by twos, right and left of the engine and took their places at the rear of the children. A platform had been erected from which Mr. Bowen took an open air service, in the middle of which the ceremony took place. Old Mr. Walton was handed a trowel and mallet. He made a short speech in which he said that it was the happiest day of his life because for a long number of years he had hoped and prayed that he might live to see the day when Haughton Green should possess a church of its own. Tears ran down his cheeks as he stepped forward and officially laid the stone. A bottle had been placed underneath containing the newspapers of the day and a document with the following statement:— "The foundation stone of this church which is to be dedicated to St. Mary the Virgin, was laid by James Walton, Esq. of Haughton Dale Mills and of Dolforgan, Montgomeryshire, on the afternoon of Saturday, April 11th in the year of our Lord 1874, in the presence of the scholars of the Church Sunday schools of Haughton Dale, St. Lawrence and Christ Church, the Ancient Order of Free and accepted Masons, the United Order of Oddfellows, the Loyal Order of Orangemen and a large concourse of people. The cost of the building of this church will be defrayed mainly by the generosity of James Walton, Esq., aforesaid, William Walton, Esq., his son and other members of the same family and the Diocesan Church Building Society. Charles James Bowen, M.D., Trinity College, Cambridge, Rector of St. Lawrence, Denton, in which parish this church is built. Rev. Charles Morris, B.A., Corpus

[1] Middleton: page 137.

136

Christ College, Oxon, Curate of the above. John Bentley and John Taylor, churchwardens of the same. William Woodley and Joseph Horsfield, sidesmen of the same. The committee for carrying out the necessary arrangements for laying the stone, besides the above-mentioned are: Thomas Kemp Walton, Charles Cooper, Peter Hulse, secretary; James Rowbotham, J. T. Hulse, James Clark, James Brown, John Mellor and James Worth. Dated, Haughton Green, in the township of Haughton, in the Parish of St. Lawrence, Denton, in the county of Lancaster, eleventh day of April, in the year of our Lord 1874 and in the 37th year of the reign of our Gracious Sovereign Queen Victoria."[1]

Most Noble Minded Men

After the ceremony, games were provided for the children in a neighbouring field, whilst the adults retired to the Iron School for a tea party. On these occasions it was customary for the Chairman to invite all persons of note to speak. Between the speeches came songs and glees performed by singers to entertain the company. All the usual compliments were paid, good wishes expressed and all was going perfectly until the new Rector of Christ Church, the Rev. W. Caine was asked to address the company. He was a strong teetotaller and took the opportunity to lament the amount of money spent in this civilised country on intoxicating drinks and more especially did he deplore the great amount of drunkenness in his own parish. He could name no less than twenty-four public houses and estimated that twenty-five to thirty thousand pounds per year were spent in them. To increase the wages of workingmen only increases drunkenness and he regretted that sometimes churches were built by people like Bass the brewer. Mr. Caine must have known that he was in the presence of some very strong Conservatives[2] and that the country's leading brewers have always been generous supporters of that party, but he was determined to campaign for total abstention. His remarks did not go unchallenged. When the Rev. J. Cumming Macdona, Rector of Cheadle and a personal friend of William Walton, rose to speak, he told the company that he had no hesitation in saying that the most noble minded men in the country were brewers. And they had done a considerable amount of good with their money. One of the first churches in the kingdom, St. Patrick's Cathedral in Dublin, had been built by Guiness.

It is interesting that this issue should have come to the surface at the Tea Party because the campaign for total abstinence had been growing

[1] *Denton & Haughton Weekly News*, 17th April, 1874.
[2] Indeed he was probably one himself. Note his reactionary attitude to workmen's wages.

since 1830 and was now extremely strong. In that year, a Conservative Government had passed a Beer Act, which relaxed restrictions on brewing to such an extent that there was a meteoric rise in drunkenness. It became a major problem which had to be tackled and the free churches gradually aligned themselves with teetotallism. The Church of England did not commit itself to teetotallism, but as time went by, some clergy espoused the cause. In Denton, the first Church of England clergyman was Mr. Caine and this produced a tense atmosphere at Christ Church. Indeed, four days after the Tea Party, a major row broke out at Christ Church's Annual Vestry meeting. Messrs. Arrundale and Taylor, the churchwardens, refused to serve any longer and handed in their resignations after making a number of complaints about their rector. A careful reading of the long newspaper account shows that a number of trivial incidents were used as pretexts for a clash of personalities and what was worrying the laymen of Christ Church more than anything else was that Mr. Caine was such a convinced teetotaller that he had started a Band of Hope! This could never be anything other than a bone of contention in a Church of England parish and Mr. Taylor[1] had objected to it being held in church so the rector had declared that he would hire a room for it![2]

On Monday, April 20th, the Vestry meeting was resumed. Mr. Woolfenden was elected as Parishioners' Warden and Mr. Hyde as Minister's Warden. Mr. Caine stayed until 1886 but he was never happy and controversy flared up on a number of issues.

The Consecration

By the beginning of 1876, St. Mary's, in some ways, such a flattering imitation of Denton Old Church, was ready to be used and services were held in it from January 19th. The consecration, however, was not held until Saturday, March 25th – the feast of the Annunciation of the Blessed Virgin Mary. The cost of the church was "something over £3,000".[3] and Mr. Walton had also given the site. Bishop Fraser would be particularly pleased to see a church with no rented pews. He had given instructions that all new churches in the diocese were to consist of free seats and free seats only. At the consecration service, which was held in the morning, he preached about being a bishop because he was just beginning his seventh year as bishop of Manchester. The summons to the office had come suddenly from Gladstone who only gave him a week to make up his mind.

[1] Mark Taylor. He was a leading *LIBERAL* in Denton, but teetotallism was too much for him.
[2] *Denton & Haughton Weekly News*, 17th April, 1874.
[3] *Denton & Haughton Weekly News*. 1st April, 1876.

After many anxious thoughts – and persuaded by his closest friends – he accepted.

Luncheon followed in the school. The Bishop thanked Mr. Walton sincerely for his great generosity and spoke out strongly against the idea of disestablishing the Church of England – a political "hot potatoe" which was being canvassed in some quarters. In the afternoon he preached at another service attended by various local friendly societies which walked to church in procession, headed by a band. A tea meeting followed in the school.

James Walton 1803-1883.

The next year old Mr. Walton was elected High Sheriff of Montgomery-shire, his distinguished career crowned by public honours. The people of Haughton Green were delighted to hear the news. If anyone deserved it, he did.

EPILOGUE

It was George Bernard Shaw who said that when he was a child he was taught that God is an English Gentleman and that all Roman Catholics go to hell. Victorian churchmen would not have found such a remark amusing. They believed it. They also believed that a good Christian is hard-working, thrifty, self-reliant and respectable, seeking to better himself in every way. Such attitudes are laudable provided they do not become the seedbed of priggishness and snobbery, but frequently they did. The Church of England in particular tended to become an elistist club for those wishing to acquire middle-class status and it seemed to Non-conformists to be little more than the Conservative Party at prayer. St. Lawrence's during the period we have studied is a good example of this and what must worry the thoughtful Christian of today is the way in which so many Churchmen put the principles of the Conservative Party first and the teaching of Christ second. Not that they did this *consciously;* they were often blandly unaware of any difference between the two!

Imagine for a few moments a typical Sunday morning congregation; the gentlemen in top hats escorting ladies wearing their best clothes. Here were the leading members of Denton's society met together to worship as God the Man who was the friend of the poor, the outcast the despised, the rejected! The Man who said that you *CANNOT* worship God and Mammon! The situation was ludicrous, but they could not see it!

Those days have gone. No one, I hope, joins a church now-a-days for the social esteem its membership carries. If it's that sort of thing you are after, you can join the Freemasons or a prestigeous golf club. This leaves the Church free to do the work to which Christ calls it. Like Him, we side with the have-nots of this world. We are not afraid to be called nigger-lovers, left-wingers or do-gooders. We reject a money-orientated view of society in which the wealthiest people are looked upon as the most 'success-ful', whilst two-thirds of the world goes hungry. Our job is to turn such attitudes upside down and we must see to it that those young people who join our churches put Christ's teaching *first* and criticise everything else in the light of it. The Christian Revolution is the most thorough-going man-kind can experience and the real joy of being a Christian only comes to those who know what it means to leave self behind and follow him.

BIBLIOGRAPHY

Immediate Sources

Booker, The Rev. J.: A History of the Ancient Chapel of Denton (Chetham Society 1855).

George Chandler: William Roscoe of Liverpool (1753–1831) (Batsford 1953).

Denton: Registers of the Parish of, 1695–1757 (Printed for the Lancashire Parish Register Society, 1913).

Farthing, T. N.: Six Sermons (London: Bemrose & Sons, 23, Old Bailey: and Derby 1889).

Grindon, L. H.: Joseph Sidebotham (A Memoir). Printed by Palmer and Howe, 73–77 Princess Street, Manchester, for Private Circulation, 1886.

Heywood, O.: A Narrative of The Holy Life and Happy Death of that Reverend, Faithful and Zealous Man of God and Minister of The Gospel of Jesus Christ, Mr. John Angier. (Printed for Thomas Parkhurst, at the Bible and Three Crowns, at the Lower End of Cheapside, near Mercers Chappel, 1683). Second edition, 1685. Re-published by the Chetham Society in 1937.

Higson, John: The Gorton Historical Register (Droylsden: published by John Higson, Market Street, 1852).

Jackson, H.: Stray Thoughts (George Booth, Market Street, Hyde, 1853).

Middleton, T.: Annals of Hyde and District (1899).

Middleton, T.: History of Hyde (1901).

Middleton, T.: Historical sketch of Denton Old Church (1931).

Middleton, T.: The History of Denton and Haughton (Hyde: J. Andrews & Co. Ltd., 1936).

Parr Greswell, W.: Memoirs of Angelus Politianus 1801. Second editions 1805 (greatly augmented).

Parr Greswell, W.: Annals of Parisian Typography (1818).

Parr Greswell, W.: Monastery of St. Werburgh (Henry Smith, St. Ann's Square, 1823).

Parr Greswell, W.: Monastery of St. Werburgh and Collected Poems (1832).

Parr Greswell, W.: View of the Early Parisian Greek Press (1833).

Raynes, Francis (Capt.) "Appeal to the Public" (London 1817).

Rose, E. A.:   Methodism in Ashton-under-Lyne
                      1. 1740–1797 (1967).
                      2. 1797–1914 (1969, J. Andrew & Co.).
St. Mary's, Market Street, Denton, Souvenir Brochure 1963.
St. Mary's Catholic Church and School Centenary Booklet, 1869–1969.
Wainwright, J.   Memories of Marple (1898)

Magazines and Newspapers
The Gentleman's Magazine.
The Monthly Review.
Ashton Reporter (1855 – The Present Day).
North Cheshire Herald (1860–1960, except 1897).
Denton, Haughton & District Weekly News (March 30th, 1872 – Oct. 16th, 1875).
Denton Examiner (October 23rd, 1875 – August, 1892).
Manchester Mercury.

Unpublished Sources
Denton, Registers of the Parish of:

Baptisms:	1695–1723, Volume 1.
Marriages and Burials:	1724–1757, Volume 2.
Baptisms:	1813–1829
	1829–1837
	1837–1853
	1854–1871
	1871–1883
Marriages:	1854–1905
Burials:	1813–1842
	1842–1873

Jarratt, Shirley: The Operation of the Old Poor Law in Denton and Chorlton-on-Medlock, 1780–1900. (In Denton Public Library).

Rate Book-cum-Scrap
    Book: Mid 19th century. (In Denton Public Library).

Overseers' Account
    Book: 1751–1799   In one volume.
Chapel Wardens
    Account Book: 1788–1799   (In Denton Public Library).
Denton Constable's
    Account Book: 1789–1819 and 1830–31 and 1866–69. (In Denton Public Library).

Wainwright, Joel:	A Foolscap Manuscript of 25 pages written as a Letter to the Rev. W. Greswell, Rector of Doddington, Somerset (a grandson of William Parr Greswell) dated Dec. 1st, 1896. This is now in the possession of Mr. R. E. Greswell of Bicknoller, Taunton, a great-great-grandson of W.P.G. (Copy in Denton Public Library).

General Sources

Bell, P. M. H.:	Disestablishment in Ireland and Wales (S.P.C.K. 1969).
Burgess, H. J.:	Enterprise in Education, S.P.C.K. 1958. (The story of the National Society).
Burgon, J. W.:	Lives of Twelve Good Men (1888). (Contains a chapter on Richard Greswell).
Chadwick, O.:	The Victorian Church, Volumes I & II. (London, Adam and Charles Black, 1970).
Pevsner, N.:	The Buildings of England: South Lancashire. (Penguin, 1969).
Sanders, J.:	Manchester. (Ruper Hart-Davies, 1967).
Swindells, G.A.	The Strines Journal. (An Appreciation, The Marple Antiquarian Society, 1972).
Trevelyan, O. M.:	English Social History. (Longman, Green & Co., 1944).

APPENDIX I

THIS IS the last Will and Testament of me William Parr Greswell, of Denton in the County of Lancaster, Clerk. I give to my Son, the Reverend William Greswell, Rector of Kilve-cum-Stringston, Somersetshire, his Heirs and Assignes, all my Freehold Houses and Hereditaments, situate in Salford, in the County of Lancaster, and formerly the property of Mr. Thomas Heamer – I also give to my said son, William, all my Estate and Interest in certain lands and Hereditaments situate at Quick, in Saddleworth, in the West Riding of the County of York, known by the name of Marled-Earth-Nook, and, now in the occupation of Joseph and Thomas Mills, Fullers and Clothiers, as joint Tenants thereof; and, also, in the perpetual water-rent and chief-rent thence arising – I give and devise my Freehold Cottages, situate at Crown Point, in Denton, aforesaid, being at present, nine in number, with their appurtenances, together with the Plot of Land adjoining to them as yet unbuilt upon, to my three Sons, William, Richard, and Clement Greswell, their heirs and Assignes, for ever, as Tenants in common, and not as joint-Tenants – I give and bequeath to the Reverend Clement Greswell, my dear Son last mentioned, now Rector of Tortworth, in the County of Gloucester, and to his Heirs, Executors, Administrators, and Assignes, all those my Five several Messuages or Dwelling Houses, with their Appurtenances which are situate in Great Ducie Street, Strangeways, in the Township of Cheetham, County of Lancaster, and subject to an annual Ground-or-Chief-Rent, payable to the Right Honourable, the Earl of Ducie, for and during the yet unexpired portion of the original Term of Nine Hundred and Ninety Nine years. To the Reverend Edward Greswell, Fellow of Corpus Christi College, Oxford, I bequeath the distinct sum of Five Hundred Pounds, now lying at Interest, on Mortgage, or other Security, given to my Son, the Reverend Richard Greswell, of the City of Oxford, and which money he now holds in Trust for me; and this, I say, I give, exclusively to Edward, together with any Interest, which may happen to be due thereon, at the time of my decease. And, as to the Residul of my Estate and Property, whether real or personal, and all other sums of money, belonging to me, and not before mentioned, whether placed out on Mortgages of Land, or of Turnpike Roads, invested in the Public Funds, or on any other Securities whatsoever, together with monies in any Bank, appertaining to me, or found in my possession, at the time of my decease; and, also, all my Books, Household Goods, Farming-Stock, Plate, and any other description of Property, whatsoever and wheresoever to me belonging, I give the same to my Four

Sons, William, Edward, Richard, and Clement, now surviving, share and share alike, with full power to keep or sell, divide or otherwise dispose of the same, or any part thereof, for their equal and mutual benefit, as they, or the Major part of them, may think proper – And, of this my last will, hereby revoking all former Wills by me made, I constitute and appoint my Sons, William, Richard and Clement, and, also William Sidebotham, of Werneth, in Cheshire, Esq., the Executors.

The witness whereof, I have hereunto set my hand and seal, this Eighth day of March, in the year of our Lord One thousand Eight Hundred and Forty-five.

WILLIAM PARR GRESWELL.

Signed, Sealed, published and declared, by
the said Testator, and witnessed by us, in
his presence and the presence of each other;
JAMES BOOTH
THOMAS BOOTH
RALPH BOARDMAN.

APPENDIX II

THIS IS the Last Will and Testament of me John Lees Senr. of Denton in the parish of Manchester in the County of Lancaster Yeoman. Calling to mind the uncertainty of Life DO make publish and ordain this my said last Will and Testament in manner and form following that is to say:

First it is my Will and mind and I do hereby Order direct and appoint that all my just and honest Debts together with my funeral expenses and the Charges of proving this my last Will be all first paid and discharged by my Executors hereafter named out of my personal or real Estate. and Effects. AND THEN I do hereby give and bequeath to my Daughter Mary all those Goods and things and in the manner prescribed in a paper given by her Mother. AND then I give to my Son Samuel my large Bible and to Esther his Daughter One Guinea Sterling AND THEN I do hereby give and bequeath the yearly rents issues and profits arising from my New House and garden at the East end of the said new house standing and being on the side of the Chapelgreen in Denton aforesaid to my Daughter Mary during her Natural Life to enter possession at my Decease and after her Death I give the said House and garden to her Children equally amongst them all and their heirs for ever AND as for and concerning my lands in freehold lying and being near the side of the Town Lane in Denton aforesaid I do hereby give and bequeath the said Lands and premises before mentioned with all my building erected hereon with their appurtenances to my Son John and his heirs for ever to enter possession at my Death He paying as a Charge upon the said Estate being Mortgaged the sum of One hundred and forty pounds of Lawfull Brittish money.

Also I give to my Son John the rest of my household Goods and husbandry tools for his good behaviour to me also I give to him in the behalf of Esther his Daughter for her use a note of Nine Guineas which now given by my Daughter Mary also my Cow if I have one for her use. THEN I give to my Son Samuel all my wearing apparel. AND THEN as for and concerning all those my lands and premises lying and being in Boothstown of Worsley in the Parish of Eccles in the County of Lancaster and my Three Cottages or Old buildings standing and being in Denton aforesaid and now inhabited by Hannah Shawcross, John Stopford and Jane Taylor, Widow I hereby charge those my lands and premises together with my said Cottages or Old buildings for the payment of Six hundred and Forty-five pounds. One hundred and ninety pounds of the said sum to be paid by my Executors to my Daughter Mary at the end of twelve months next after my decease and the rest of the money Charged upon the said Lands and Cottages towards the payment of the Debts charged thereon AND I hereby give my Executors power and authority to sell or dispose of all or any part of the said Lands and premises and Cottages at their discretion towards the paying all the Debts charged thereon AND THEN if anything remain when the Debts are all paid I give the rest of any there shall be to my Son Samuel and his heirs. THEN all the remainder of my personal or real Estate and effects if any there shall be I give to my Three Executors equally amongst them share and share alike if there be any Interest due to me from any of my Children Upon Note or Bill or Bond at my Death then that money shall be paid into my Executors' Hands towards the discharging of Debts if any there be. It is my Will and Mind and I do hereby direct and appoint that my Executors and the Survivor of them his or their Exors Admors and Asses shall be fully indemnified and saved harmless by and out of my Estate and Effects of and from all cost charges and damages whatsoever which they or any of them shall or may lay out or be put unto about the execution of this my last Will and LASTLY I do hereby Nominate constitute and appoint John my Son and Samuel my Son and James Oldham my Son in Law joint Executors of this my last WILL and Testament hopeing they will perform and fulfill the same as my trust is in them reposed. IN WITNESS whereof I the said John Lees the Testator to this my last Will and Testament have set my Hand and Seal the Nineteenth Day of November in the Year of Our Lord one Thousand and Seven hundred and Eighty five.

Signed sealed published and Declared
by the said John Lees the Testator as   JOHN LEES
and for his last Will and Testament.
In the presence of us and who in his
presence and at his request and in the
sight and presence of each other have
subscribed our names and Witness   The whole charge of my Son
hereto   John being 140 £
                                           and my Son
                                           Samuels being 645 pounds

Francis Brelsford
John Bailey
John Bottomley
All Interliniations and erasiers first made
The 9th day of June 1786, John Lees, Samuel Lees, and James Oldham, the extors within named were sworn in common form before me,
W. Bowness, Surrogate.

APPENDIX III

LETTER FROM JAMES RALSTON TO THE EDITORS OF THE STRINES JOURNAL

A FACSIMILE of this beautiful letter, showing the small, clear hand-writing, appears in Joel Wainwright's "Memoirs of Marple". It is written in the third person, like the letter from George Hyde Clarke printed in Chapter II. Now-a-days, we only use letters in the third person on rare occasions. A formal wedding invitation is a letter in the third person and a reply to it should be in the same form.

Disley, near Stockport, April 5th, 1854.

J. Ralston is much obliged to the Editors of the *Strines Journal* for their kindness in lending him so many numbers at once of that work, with which both as respects the literary and decorative parts he has been highly enter-tained and pleased, never more so.– When he resided at Reddish Mill, and Denton Chapel being the nearest place of worship, he frequently attended the afternoon service there; more frequently perhaps on account of having read in the *Monthly Review* for Oct. 1801 a very favourable criticism on Memoirs of and Translations from certain Italian writers of the 15th and 16th centuries by the Rev. Parr Greswell, Minister of the said Chapel, (so exquisitely delineated in Your Journal, and which even Yet in his way home from Manchester he frequently makes a point of visiting) and was proud of having the privilege of seeing and hearing such a gentleman; and was no less so after the lapse of many years on welcoming his son the Rev. W. Greswell to Disley to which place he was appointed Minister whilst R held the office of Churchwarden. Many were the acts of kindness which the Minister performed for his officer: accompanied him in all his excursions in search of subscriptions for a Church Clock, tendered him the use of his bath. Recorded his services in the town's books in a more flattering manner and at greater length than had ever been done for any former Churchwarden of the same place when resigning his office.

William was an author too, and as a remembrance presented the warden with a copy of his last work in two large volumes octave, printed at the University and entitled "A Commentary on the order for the burial of the Dead etc." on the fly leaf of which he wrote – Presented to James Ralston by the Rev. W. Greswell April 10th 1837 – so that J. R. has great cause to be interested in all that relates to Denton Chapel and the family of Greswell, and has taken the liberty to make an extract from Your article thereon. – Speaking on other matters, like the "northern Tourist" he would have no guide to any place on the surface of the earth at least in Great Britain or Ireland no matter how high.

About the year 1805 himself and an Artist, made an excursion from Strines to Furness Abbey, the Lakes of Lancashire, Cumberland, Westmoreland, and Dumbartonshire; Glen Crow, Stirling, Edinburgh, etc., 1019 miles every inch on foot, which occupied 36 days and during which the Artist made 109 excellent sketches; whilst the other read through and delivered extempore lectures on Milton's Paradise Lost, the result of which was that there ought to be published what would now be called a family Milton. Though they generally put up at the best Inns the whole expense for both did not much exceed £10. The favourite beverage of one was water; the other would absolutely drink nothing else. Their shortest days journey was 14 miles, their longest 62; the time required for making a sketch varied from a $\frac{1}{4}$ to $3\frac{1}{2}$ hours. Drumnabrig was one of the latter, and taken the day on which they walked the 62 miles.

You are fortunate in having such a correspondent as Paul – have never seen anything better than his No. 1 nor read anything better on the subject than his directions. Though the Artist above alluded to preferred a reed to any kind of a pen, but they are not always to be had. His nursery for them was at the mouth of a tunnel between Marple Aqueduct and Hatherlow.

But the messenger is waiting and the Journals have already been detained too long.

APPENDIX IV

SAMUEL SIDLEY (1829–1896)

THE FINE water colour painting of Denton Old Chapel from the north-west now hanging in St. Lawrence's Church is by Samuel Sidley who was born in Yorkshire in 1829. He studied art first in Manchester and then at the Royal Academy Schools, London, being admitted there on December 19th, 1854. This painting of Denton Old Chapel must have been done between 1853 and 1862. He seems to have set up his easel on the site of the old Chapelhouse which was taken down in that year and he clearly shows Robert Hyde's box pew standing on its two stilts. This was removed in the 1862 Restoration. But where are the cottages abutting the west end of the chapel? And where is the old School which could be seen from this viewpoint beyond the lych gate and was used as a machine shop until it was demolished in 1867? He must have exercised artistic licence and left them out in the interests of good compositon!

He first exhibited at the Royal Academy in 1855 when his address was given as 8, Mottram Street, Hyde; sending a picture called "An Ancient Mariner". It was as a portrait painter that he became well known and he obtained commission from leading members of society. His picture of Bishop Colenso is in the National Portrait Gallery. On July 9th, 1896 he died in Kensington.[1]

[1] Dictionary of National Biography.

APPENDIX V

JAMES WALTON of Dolforgan, Kerry, was remarkable for his inventive genius. Like Brindley and Arkwright and other great leaders of industry who have established the supremacy of England as a manufacturing nation, he was a man of marked individuality of character, clearness of mental vision, strength of will, and steadfastness of purpose, and he has left behind him a long roll of original ideas, many of which, carried into practice, have assisted greatly in increasing the productive powers of the great cotton-spinning trade. He was the son of Mr. Isaac Walton, a merchant and friezer of woollen goods, and was born at the Stubbins, Ripponden, Yorkshire, April 15th, 1803. While working with his father he noticed the defects of the somewhat primitive friezing machine then in use, and set to work to improve it. He was then from eighteen to twenty years of age. To enable himself to carry out his experiments he removed to a small workshop near the North Bridge, Halifax, where he constructed the first improved friezing machine. About 1824 he removed to larger premises at Sowerby Bridge. To meet the demand that arose, he built a considerable number of these machines for the supply of the then famous Petersham cloth, and for two years, that is, while that cloth continued in fashion, they were kept continuously working day and night. This first success brought him a considerable fortune; but not satisfied with it he continued his experiments, the result being that in 1834 he invented a series of machines for raising the pile of woollen fabrics by means of wire cards, in place of the vegetable teazles formerly employed for that purpose. He also constructed at Sowerby Bridge the largest planing machine which had up to that time been attempted in this country. About 1836 he went to Manchester, and entered into partnership with Messrs. Parr & Curtis, the owners of the original American card-setting machine, who carried on the business of patent cardmaking in Store Street, London Road, and subsequently in Ancoats, where the extensive machine-making works of Messrs. Parr & Curtis are still carried on. Mr. Walton invented several beautiful and ingenious contrivances for the improvement of the card-setting machine, which he brought to its present high state of speed and perfection. It was, indeed, for a long time, and to some extent still is, one of the most interesting and attractive sights in the cotton industry of Lancashire. Amidst all the wonders of mechanical science it stands almost unrivalled as an example of rapidity and precision of mechanical action, and many have watched its movements and stood lost in wonder at the almost sentient activity of this little automaton, which hour after hour works on with unvarying certainty of action. About this time he also invented and patented an improved foundation for the backs of wire cards, namely layers of cloth and india-rubber connected together in lieu of leather. This invention was contested, and became the subject of long and expensive litigation, the suits of Walton v. Potter & Horsfall, which extended from 1839 to 1843. Mr. Walton then made a vow that he would never afterwards enter a Court of Justice, a vow which he religiously observed even while he was High Sheriff of Montgomeryshire. The rubber as then manufactured by the process of mastication proving defective, Mr. Walton again set to work and remedied the defect by the invention of a series of ingenious machines and processes which enabled him to produce an endless sheet of rubber without mastication. Having succeeded, he would not trust himself again to the uncertain protection of the patent laws of the time, but selected trustworthy men to work in these departments, which he kept strictly under lock and key for about ten years, during which, and before the secret leaked out, he was able not only to recoup himself the great cost of the previous patent trials, but to accumulate a large fortune out of the advantages his cards possessed over those of other manufacturers. His process is now almost universally adopted as the most perfect method of making wire cards for cotton spinning. After some time Mr. Walton's partnership with Messrs. Parr & Curtis was dissolved. In 1853 he established the large card-manufacturing concern at Haughton Dale, near Manchester, the largest of its kind probably in the world, where he and his sons effected many other important improvements, which greatly reduced the price of cards, the cotton-spinner of to-day paying about one-fourth of the prices formerly charged. Among numerous other inventions by Mr. Walton, not already mentioned, may be named the machines for cutting and facing the various tappets and double twill wheels, the first practical wire stop-motion for machines, a new system of wire-drawing, wire-testing, and wire brush-making, and the patent rolled angular wire, all of which attest the fertility of his inventive genius. It is satisfactory to be able to add that he himself was permitted to reap the reward of his own patient toil, talent and industry, and that he amassed a large fortune. He resided some years at Compstall, in Derbyshire. Subsequently, he, about eighteen or twenty years ago, purchased the Cwmllecoediog estate, Mallwyd, and took up his residence there. He afterwards, in 1868, purchased the mansion and estate of Dolforgan, Kerry, where he principally dwelt the rest of his life, having retired from active business some years before. He served the office of Sheriff of Montgomeryshire in 1877. Mr. Walton was of a very quiet, retiring dispositon, and could never be induced to appear as a public man. He was a very liberal benefactor to institutions of a religious, educational and charitable character, and often gave away large sums anonymously. He erected a large day and Sunday school at Haughton, and in 1876 he and his son, Mr. William Walton, founded and endowed a church at the same place at a cost of £4,000. A little before his death he contributed £1,000 towards the restoration of Kerry Church. He died at Dolforgan, November 5th, 1883, aged eighty years, and was buried in Kerry churchyard, being, in fact, the first to be interred in a portion of land just added from the Dolforgan estate. Mr. Walton's only surviving sons, William (who still carries on the business at Haughton) and Phillip, inherit some of Mr. Walton's inventive genius, Mr. Phillip Walton having originated and established the now important industry of linoleum floorcloth, as well as that of Lincrusta-Walton wall decoration. – *Times; Oswestry Advertiser; Halifax Guardian,* etc.). – from "Montgomeryshire Worthies" (1885).

INDEX

WILLIAM PARR GRESWELL (1765 1854) MARRIED ANNE HAGUE (1763 1841)
IN
1794
— THEIR CHILDREN —

THOMAS HEAMER
Born 26th April, 1795

Educated by his father

Master of Blue Coat School, Manchester

Died March 9th, 1819 Buried in St. Lawrence's graveyard in the family grave

WILLIAM
Born 10th July, 1796

Educated by his father Then attended Manchester School

Enters Oxford 1817 (Hulmian Exibition)

B.A. 1818 (First Class)

Fellow of Balliol M.A. 1820 ordained

Incumbent of St. Mary, Disley, Cheshire, 1829 1837

Rector of Kilve, Somerset, 1837 1877

1838 Married Mary Ann Harrison

Died 1877

3 sons and 7 daughters

EDWARD
Born August 3rd, 1797

Educated by his father Then attended Manchester School

Enters Brasenose Oxford, 1815

B.A. 1818 First Class in Classics and Mathematics

M.A. 1822

Fellow of Corpus Christi, 1823

1825 made Deacon

1826 ordained Priest

B.D. 1830

College Tutor, 1822 1834

Died in his rooms at Oxford on 29th June, 1869. Buried in cloisters of Corpus Christi

SARAH
Born 11th February, 1799

Died 16th June, 1802 Buried in family grave in St. Lawrence's churchyard

RICHARD
Born 22nd July, 1800

Educated by his father

Enters Oxford

B.A. 1822 First Class in Classics and Mathematics

M.A. 1825

Fellow and Tutor of Worcester College from 1824

B.D. 1836

1836 Married Joana Julia Armitriding

2 daughters

Died July 22nd, 1881 (His birthday)

CHARLES
Born 27th February, 1802

Educated by his father

Surgeon of Strangeways

Died 8th May, 1844 Buried in family grave in St. Lawrence's Churchyard

FRANCIS HAGUE
Born 24th August, 1803

Educated by his father

1826 Lit. Hum. 2nd Class

Fellow of Brazenose

1829 Ordained as Assistant Curate to his father at Denton Chapel

1830 died January 27th, William takes funeral

Buried in family grave

SARAH ANNE
Born 14th April, 1805

Died 2nd August, 1822 Buried in family grave

CLEMENT
Born 9th January, 1809

Educated by his father

Oxford, Corpus Christi

1827 B.A. (1st Class)

1830 40 Fellow of Oriel

1831 M.A.

1840 Rector of Tortworth in Cloucestershire,

Married Elizabeth Karslake of N. Devon

Numerous children

Died 1882